经典的回声·ECHO OF CLASSICS

楚辞选
SELECTED ELEGIES OF THE STATE OF CHU

屈　原　著

杨宪益　戴乃迭　译

By Qu Yuan
Translated by
Yang Xianyi and Gladys Yang

外文出版社
FOREIGN LANGUAGES PRESS

图书在版编目（CIP）数据

楚辞选/（战国）屈原著；杨宪益，戴乃迭英译.
－北京：外文出版社，2001.8
（经典的回声）
ISBN 7-119-02890-1

Ⅰ.楚…　Ⅱ.①屈…　②杨…　③戴…　Ⅲ.英语－对照读物，
楚辞－汉、英　Ⅳ.H319.4:I

中国版本图书馆 CIP 数据核字（2001）第 042715 号

外文出版社网址：
　http://www.flp.com.cn
外文出版社电子信箱：
　info@flp.com.cn
　sales@flp.com.cn

经典的回声（汉英对照）

楚辞选

作　　者	（战国）屈　原	
译　　者	杨宪益　戴乃迭	
责任编辑	余冰清	
封面设计	席恒青	
印刷监制	张国祥	
出版发行	外文出版社	
社　　址	北京市百万庄大街24号	邮政编码　100037
电　　话	（010）68320579（总编室）	
	（010）68329514／68327211（推广发行部）	
印　　刷	三河市汇鑫印务有限公司	
经　　销	新华书店/外文书店	
开　　本	大32开（850×1168毫米）	字　　数　50千字
印　　数	5001－8000册	印　　张　5.5
版　　次	2004年10月第1版第2次印刷	
装　　别	平装	
书　　号	ISBN 7-119-02890-1	
定　　价	10.00元	

出 版 前 言

本社专事外文图书的编辑出版,几十年来用英文翻译出版了大量的中国文学作品和文化典籍,上自先秦,下迄现当代,力求全面而准确地反映中国文学及中国文化的基本面貌和灿烂成就。这些英译图书均取自相关领域著名的、权威的作品,英译则出自国内外译界名家。每本图书的编选、翻译过程均极其审慎严肃,精雕细琢,中文作品及相应的英译版本均堪称经典。

我们意识到,这些英译精品,不单有对外译介的意义,而且对国内英文学习者、爱好者及英译工作者,也是极有价值的读本。为此,我们对这些英译精品做了认真的遴选,编排成汉英对照的形式,陆续推出,以飨读者。

外文出版社

Publisher's Note

Foreign Languages Press is dedicated to the editing, translating and publishing of books in foreign languages. Over the past several decades it has published, in English, a great number of China's classics and records as well as literary works from the Qin down to modern times, in the aim to fully display the best part of the Chinese culture and its achievements. These books in the original are famous and authoritative in their respective fields, and their English translations are masterworks produced by notable translators both at home and abroad. Each book is carefully compiled and translated with minute precision. Consequently, the English versions as well as their Chinese originals may both be rated as classics.

It is generally considered that these English translations are not only significant for introducing China to the outside world but also useful reading materials for domestic English learners and translators. For this reason, we have carefully selected some of these books, and will publish them successively in Chinese-English bilingual form.

Foreign Languages Press

目　　录
CONTENTS

楚 辞 选

SELECTED ELEGIES OF
THE STATE OF CHU

离　骚

帝高阳之苗裔兮,朕皇考曰伯庸。

摄提贞于孟陬兮,惟庚寅吾以降。

皇览揆余初度兮,肇锡余以嘉名:

名余曰正则兮,字余曰灵均。

纷吾既有此内美兮,又重之以修能。

扈江离与辟芷兮,纫秋兰以为佩。

汨余若将不及兮,恐年岁之不吾与。

朝搴阰之木兰兮,夕揽洲之宿莽。

日月忽其不淹兮,春与秋其代序。

惟草木之零落兮,恐美人之迟暮。

LI SAO

A Prince am I of Ancestry renowned,
Illustrious Name my royal Sire hath found.
When Sirius did in Spring its Light display,
A Child was born, and Tiger marked the Day.
When first upon my Face my Lord's Eye glanced,
For me auspicious Names he straight advanced,
Denoting that in me Heaven's Marks divine
Should with the Virtues of the Earth combine.
With lavished innate Qualities indued,
By Art and Skill my Talents I renewed;
Angelic Herbs and sweet Selineas too,
And Orchids late that by the Water grew,
I wove for Ornament; till creeping Time,
Like Water flowing, stole away my Prime.
Magnolias of the Glade I plucked at Dawn,
At Eve beside the Stream took Winter-thorn.
Without Delay the Sun and Moon sped fast,
In swift Succession Spring and Autumn passed;
The fallen Flowers lay scattered on the Ground,
The Dusk might fall before my Dream was found.

不抚壮而弃秽兮,何不改此度?

乘骐骥以驰骋兮,来吾道夫先路!

昔三后之纯粹兮,固众芳之所在;

杂申椒与菌桂兮,岂维纫夫蕙茝?

彼尧舜之耿介兮,既遵道而得路;

何桀纣之猖披兮,夫唯捷径以窘步。

惟夫党人之偷乐兮,路幽昧以险隘。

岂余身之惮殃兮,恐皇舆之败绩!

忽奔走以先后兮,及前王之踵武。

荃不察余之中情兮,反信谗而齌怒。

余固知謇謇之为患兮,忍而不能舍也。

指九天以为正兮,夫唯灵修之故也!

Had I not loved my Prime and spurned the Vile,
Why should I not have changed my former Style?
My Chariot drawn by Steeds of Race divine
I urged; to guide the King my sole Design.

Three ancient Kings there were so pure and true
That round them every fragrant Flower grew;
Cassia and Pepper of the Mountain-side
With Melilotus white in Clusters vied.
Two Monarchs then, who high Renown received,
Followed the kingly Way, their Goal achieved.
Two Princes proud by Lust their Reign abused,
Sought easier Path, and their own Steps confused.
The Faction for illicit Pleasure longed;
Dreadful their Way where hidden Perils thronged.
Danger against myself could not appal,
But feared I lest my Sovereign's Sceptre fall.

Forward and back I hastened in my Quest,
Followed the former Kings, and took no Rest.
The Prince my true Integrity defamed,
Gave Ear to Slander, high his Anger flamed;
Integrity I knew could not avail,
Yet still endured; my Lord I would not fail.
Celestial Spheres my Witness be on high,
I strove but for His Sacred Majesty.
Twas first to me gave his plighted Word,

曰黄昏以为期兮,羌中道而改路。

初既与余成言兮,后悔遁而有他。

余既不难夫离别兮,伤灵修之数化。

余既滋兰之九畹兮,又树蕙之百亩。

畦留夷与揭车兮,杂杜衡与芳芷。

冀枝叶之峻茂兮,愿俟时乎吾将刈。

虽萎绝其亦何伤兮,哀众芳之芜秽!

众皆竞进以贪婪兮,凭不厌乎求索。

羌内恕己以量人兮,各兴心而嫉妒。

忽驰骛以追逐兮,非余心之所急。

老冉冉其将至兮,恐修名之不立。

朝饮木兰之坠露兮,夕餐秋菊之落英。

苟余情其信姱以练要兮,长顑颔亦何伤!

But soon repenting other Counsel heard.
For me Departure could arouse no Pain;
I grieved to see his royal Purpose vain.

Nine Fields of Orchids at one Time I grew,
For Melilot a hundred Acres too,
And fifty Acres for the Azalea bright,
The Rumex fragrant and the Lichen white.
I longed to see them yielding Blossoms rare,
And thought in Season due the Spoil to share.
I did not grieve to see them die away,
But grieved because midst Weeds they did decay.

Insatiable in Lust and Greediness
The Faction strove, and tired not of Excess;
Themselves condoning, others they'd decry,
And steep their Hearts in envious Jealousy.

Insatiably they seized what they desired,
It was not that to which my Heart aspired.
As old Age unrelenting hurried near,
Lest my fair Name should fail was all my Fear.
Dew from Magnolia Leaves I drank at Dawn,
At Eve for Food were Aster Petals borne;
And loving thus the Simple and the Fair,
How should I for my sallow Features care?
With gathered Vines I strung Valeria white,
And mixed with blue Wistaria Petals bright,

揽木根以结茝兮，贯薜荔之落蕊。

矫菌桂以纫蕙兮，索胡绳之缅缅。

謇吾法夫前修兮，非世俗之所服。

虽不周于今之人兮，愿依彭咸之遗则。

长太息以掩涕兮，哀民生之多艰。

余虽好修姱以鞿羁兮，謇朝谇而夕替。

既替余以蕙纕兮，又申之以揽茝。

亦余心之所善兮，虽九死其犹未悔！

怨灵修之浩荡兮，终不察夫民心。

众女嫉余之蛾眉兮，谣诼谓余以善淫。

固时俗之工巧兮，偭规矩而改错；

背绳墨以追曲兮，竞周容以为度。

忳郁邑余侘傺兮，吾独穷困乎此时也。

宁溘死以流亡兮，余不忍为此态也！

And Melilotus matched with Cassia sweet,
With Ivy green and Tendrils long to meet.
Life I adapted to the ancient Way,
Leaving the Manners of the present Day;
Thus unconforming to the modern Age,
The Path I followed of a bygone Sage.

Long did I sigh and wipe away my Tears,
To see my People bowed by Griefs and Fears.
Though I my Gifts enhanced and curbed my Pride,
At Morn they'd mock me, would at Eve deride;
First cursed that I Angelica should wear,
Then cursed me for my Melilotus fair.
But since my Heart did love such Purity,
I'd not regret a thousand Deaths to die.

I marvel at the Folly of the King,
So heedless of his People's Suffering.
They envied me my mothlike Eyebrows fine,
And so my Name his Damsels did malign.
Truly to Craft alone their Praise they paid,
The Square in Measuring they disobeyed;
The Use of common Rules they held debased;
With Confidence their crooked Lines they traced.

In Sadness plunged and sunk in deepest Gloom,
Alone I drove on to my dreary Doom.
In Exile rather would I meet my End,
Than to the Abaseness of their Ways descend.

鸷鸟之不群兮，自前世而固然。

何方圜之能周兮，夫孰异道而相安！

屈心而抑志兮，忍尤而攘诟。

伏清白以死直兮，固前圣之所厚。

悔相道之不察兮，延伫乎吾将反。

回朕车以复路兮，及行迷之未远。

步余马于兰皋兮，驰椒丘且焉止息。

进不入以离尤兮，退将复修吾初服。

制芰荷以为衣兮，集芙蓉以为裳。

不吾知其亦已兮，苟余情其信芳。

高余冠之岌岌兮，长余佩之陆离。

芳与泽其杂糅兮，唯昭质其犹未亏。

Remote the Eagle spurns the common Range,
Not deigns since Time began its Way to change;
A Circle fits not with a square Design;
Their different Ways could not be merged with
  mine.
Yet still my Heart I checked and curbed my Pride,
Their Blame endured and their Reproach beside.
To die for Righteousness alone I sought,
For this was what the ancient Sages taught.

I failed my former Errors to discern;
I tarried long, but now I would return.
My Steeds I wheeled back to their former Way,
Lest all too long down the wrong Path I stray.
On Orchid-covered Bank I loosed my Steed,
And let him gallop by the flow'ry Mead
At Will. Rejected now and in Disgrace,
I would retire to cultivate my Grace.
With Cress Leaves green my simple Gown I made,
With Lilies white my rustic Garb did braid.
Why should I grieve to go unrecognised,
Since in my Heart Fragrance was truly prized?
My Headdress then high-pinnacled I raised,
Lengthened my Pendents, where bright Jewels
  blazed.
Others may smirch their Fragrance and bright
  Hues,
My Innocence is proof against Abuse.

忽反顾以游目兮,将往观乎四荒。

佩缤纷其繁饰兮,芳菲菲其弥章。

民生各有所乐兮,余独好修以为常。

虽体解吾犹未变兮,岂余心之可惩!

女嬃之婵媛兮,申申其詈予。

曰:"鲧婞直以亡身兮,终然殀乎羽之野。

汝何博謇而好修兮,纷独有此姱节?

薋菉葹以盈室兮,判独离而不服。

众不可户说兮,孰云察余之中情?

世并举而好朋兮,夫何茕独而不予听?"

依前圣以节中兮,喟凭心而历兹。

济沅湘以南征兮,就重华而陈词:

"启九辩与九歌兮,夏康娱以自纵。

Oft I looked back, gazed to the Distance still,
Longed in the Wilderness to roam at Will.
Splendid my Ornaments together vied,
With all the Fragrance of the Flowers beside;
All men had Pleasures in their various Ways,
My Pleasure was to cultivate my Grace.
I would not change, though they my Body rend;
How could my Heart be wrested from its End?

My Handmaid fair, with Countenance demure,
Entreated me Allegiance to abjure;
"A Hero perished in the Plain ill-starred,
Where Pigmies stayed their Plumage to discard.
Why lovest thou thy Grace and Purity,
Alone dost hold thy splendid Virtue high?
Lentile and Weeds the Prince's Chamber fill:
Why holdest thou aloof with stubborn Will?
Thou canst not one by one the Crowd persuade,
And who the Purpose of our Heart hath weighed?
Faction and Strife the World hath ever loved;
Heeding me not, why standest thou removed?"

I sought th'ancestral Voice to ease my Woe.
Alas, how one so proud could sink so low!
To barbarous South I went across the Stream;
Before the Ancient I began my Theme:
"With Odes divine there came a Monarch's Son,
Whose Revels unrestrained were never done;

不顾难以图后兮,五子用失乎家巷。

羿淫游以佚畋兮,又好射夫封狐。

固乱流其鲜终兮,浞又贪夫厥家。

浇身被服强圉兮,纵欲而不忍。

日康娱而自忘兮,厥首用夫颠陨。

夏桀之常违兮,乃遂焉而逢殃。

后辛之菹醢兮,殷宗用而不长。

"汤禹俨而只敬兮,周论道而莫差,

举贤而授能兮,循绳墨而不颇。

皇天无私阿兮,览民德焉错辅。

夫维圣哲以茂行兮,苟得用此下土。

瞻前而顾后兮,相观民之计极。

夫孰非义而可用兮,孰非善而可服?

In Antics wild, to coming Perils blind,
He fought his Brother, and his Sway declined.
The royal Archer, in his wanton Chase
For Foxes huge, his Kingdom did disgrace.
Such Wantonness predicts no happy End;
His Queen was stolen by his loyal Friend.
The Traitor's Son, clad in prodigious Might,
In Incest sinned and cared not what was right.
He revelled all his Days, forgetting all;
His Head at last in Treachery did fall.
And then the Prince, who Counsels disobeyed,
Did court Disaster, and his Kingdom fade.
A Prince his Sage in burning Cauldrons tossed;
His glorious Dynasty ere long was lost.

"But stern and pious was their ancient Sire,
And his Successor too did Faith inspire;
Exalted were the Wise, the Able used,
The Rule was kept and never was abused.
The august heaven, with unbiassed Grace,
All Men discerns, and helps the virtuous Race;
Sagacious Princes through their virtuous Deed
The Earth inherit, and their Reigns succeed.
The Past I probed, the Future so to scan,
And found these Rules that guide the Life of Man:
A Man unjust in Deed who would engage?
Whom should Men take as Guide except the Sage?
In mortal Dangers Death I have defied,

阽余身而危死兮，览余初其犹未悔，

不量凿而正枘兮，固前修以菹醢。”

曾歔欷余郁邑兮，哀朕时之不当。

揽茹蕙以掩涕兮，沾余襟之浪浪。

跪敷衽以陈辞兮，耿吾既得此中正。

驷玉虬以乘鹥兮，溘埃风余上征。

朝发轫于苍梧兮，夕余至乎县圃。

欲少留此灵琐兮，日忽忽其将暮。

吾令羲和弭节兮，望崦嵫而勿迫。

路曼曼其修远兮，吾将上下而求索。

饮余马于咸池兮，总余辔乎扶桑。

Yet could look back, and cast Regret aside.
Who strove, their Tool's Defects accounting
  nought,
Like ancient Sages were to Cauldrons brought."
Thus I despaired, my Face with sad Tears marred,
Mourning with Bitterness my Years ill-starred;
And Melilotus Leaves I took to stem
The Tears that streamed down to my Garment's
  Hem.
Soiling my Gown, to plead my Case I kneeled;
Th'ancestral Voice the Path to me revealed.

Swift jade-green Dragons, Birds with Plumage
  gold,
I harnessed to the Whirlwind, and behold,
At Daybreak from the Land of Plane-trees grey,
I came to Paradise ere close of Day.
I wished within the sacred Grove to stay,
The Sun had dropped, and Darkness wrapped the
  Way;
The Driver of the Sun I bade to stay,
Ere with the setting Rays we haste away.
The Way was long, and wrapped in Gloom did
  seem,
As I urged on to seek my vanished Dream.

The Dragons quenched their Thirst beside the Lake
Where bathed the Sun, whilst I upon the Brake

折若木以拂日兮，聊逍遥以相羊。

前望舒使先驱兮，后飞廉使奔属。

鸾皇为余先戒兮，雷师告余以未具。

吾令凤鸟飞腾兮，继之以日夜。

飘风屯其相离兮，帅云霓而来御。

纷总总其离合兮，斑陆离其上下。

吾令帝阍开关兮，倚阊阖而望予。

时暧暧其将罢兮，结幽兰而延伫，

世溷浊而不分兮，好蔽美而嫉妒。

朝吾将济于白水兮，登阆风而绁马。

忽反顾以流涕兮，哀高丘之无女。

溘吾游此春宫兮，折琼枝以继佩。

及荣华之未落兮，相下女之可诒。

Fastened my Reins; a golden Bough I sought
To brush the Sun, and tarried there in Sport.
The pale Moon's Charioteer I then bade lead,
The Master of the Winds swiftly succeed;
Before, the royal Blue Bird cleared the Way;
The Lord of Thunder urged me to delay.
I bade the Phoenix scan the Heaven wide;
But vainly Day and Night its Course it tried;
The gathering Whirlwinds drove it from my Sight,
Rushing with lowering Clouds to check my Flight;
Sifting and merging in the Firmament,
Above, below, in various Hues they went.

The Gate-keeper of Heaven I bade give Place,
But leaning on his Door he scanned my Face;
The Day grew dark, and now was nearly spent;
Idly my Orchids into Wreaths I bent.
The Virtuous and the Vile in Darkness merged;
They veiled my Virtue, by their Envy urged.
At Dawn the Waters white I left behind;
My Steed stayed be the Portals of the Wind;
Yet, gazing back, a bitter Grief I felt
That in the lofty Crag no Damsel dwelt.

I wandered eastward to the Palace green,
And Pendents sought where Jasper Boughs were
    seen,
And vowed that they, before their Splendour fade,

吾令丰隆乘云兮，求宓妃之所在。

解佩纕以结言兮，吾令蹇修以为理。

纷总总其离合兮，忽纬繣其难迁。

夕归次于穷石兮，朝濯发乎洧盘。

保厥美以骄傲兮，日康娱以淫游。

虽信美而无礼兮，来违弃而改求。

览相观于四极兮，周流乎天余乃下。

望瑶台之偃蹇兮，见有娀之佚女。

吾令鸩为媒兮，鸩告余以不好。

雄鸠之鸣逝兮，余犹恶其佻巧。

心犹豫而狐疑兮，欲自适而不可。

凤皇既受诒兮，恐高辛之先我。

As Gift should go to grace the loveliest Maid.
The Lord of Clouds I then bade mount the Sky
To seek the Stream where once the Nymph did
    lie;
As Pledge I gave my Belt of splendid Sheen,
My Councillor appointed Go-between.
Fleeting and wilful like capricious Cloud,
Her Obstinacy swift no Change allowed.
At Dusk retired she to the Crag withdrawn,
Her Hair beside the Stream she washed at Dawn.
Exulting in her Beauty and her Pride,
Pleasure she worshipped, and no Whim denied;
So fair of Form, so careless of all Grace,
I turned to take another in her place.

To Earth's Extremities I sought my Bride,
And urged my Train through all the Heaven wide
Upon a lofty Crag of jasper Green
The beauteous Princess of the West was seen.
The Falcon then I bade entreat the Maid,
But he, demurring, would my Course dissuade;
The Turtle-Dove cooed soft and off did fly,
But I mistrusted his Frivolity.
Like Whelp in Doubt, like timid Fox in Fear,
I wished to go, but wandered ever near.
With nuptial Gifts the Phoenix swiftly went;
I feared the Prince had won her ere I sent.
I longed to travel far, yet with no Bourn,

欲远集而无所止兮,聊浮游以逍遥。

及少康之未家兮,留有虞之二姚。

理弱而媒拙兮,恐导言之不固。

世溷浊而嫉贤兮,好蔽美而称恶。

闺中既以邃远兮,哲王又不寤。

怀朕情而不发兮,余焉能忍与此终古!

索蕙茅以筵篿兮,命灵氛为余占之。

曰:"两美其必合兮,孰信修而慕之?

思九州之博大兮,岂唯是其有女?"

曰:"勉远逝而无狐疑兮,孰求美而释女?

何所独无芳草兮,尔何怀乎故宇?

世幽昧以炫曜兮,孰云察余之善恶?

I could but wander aimless and forlorn.
Before the young King was in Marriage bound,
The Royal Sisters Twain might still be found;
My Plea was weak, my Mission was but frail;
I knew that my Demand could not avail.

The World in Dark, and envious of my Grace;
They veil my Virtue and the Evil praise.
Thy Chamber dark lies in Recesses deep,
Sagacious Prince, risest thou not from Sleep?
My Zeal unknown the Prince would not descry;
How could I bear this harsh Eternity?

With Mistletoe and Herbs of magic Worth,
I urged the Witch the Future to show forth.
"If Two attain Perfection they must meet,
But who is there that would thy Virtue greet?
Far the Nine Continents their Realm display;
Why here to seek thy Bride doth thou delay?
Away!"she cried, "Set craven Doubt aside,
If Beauty's sought, there's none hath with thee
    vied.
What Place is there where Orchids flower not fair?
Why is thy native Land thy single Care?

"Now darkly lies the World in Twilight's Glow,
Who doth your Defects and your Virtue know?
Evil and Good herein are reconciled;
The Crowd alone hath Nought but is defiled.

民好恶其不同兮，惟此党入其独异。

户服艾以盈要兮，谓幽兰其不可佩。

览察草木其犹未得兮，岂珵美之能当？

苏粪壤以充帏兮，谓申椒其不芳。"

欲从灵氛之吉占兮，心犹豫而狐疑。

巫咸将夕降兮，怀椒糈而要之。

百神翳其备降兮，九疑缤其并迎。

皇剡剡其扬灵兮，告余以吉故。

曰："勉升降以上下兮，求矩矱之所同。

汤、禹严而求合兮，挚、咎繇而能调。

苟中情其好修兮，又何必用夫行媒？

说操筑于傅岩兮，武丁用而不疑。

吕望之鼓刀兮，遭周文而得举。

With stinking Mugwort girt upon their Waist,
They curse the others for their Orchids chaste;
Ignorant thus in Choice of Fragrance rare,
Rich Ornaments how could they fitly wear?
With Mud and Filth they fill their Pendent Bag;
Cursing the Pepper sweet, they brawl and brag,"
Although the Witches Counsel I held good,
In foxlike Indecision still I stood.
At Night the Wizard great made his Descent,
And meeting him spiced Rice I did present.
The Angels came, shading with Wings the Sky;
From Mountains wild the Deities drew nigh.
With regal Splendour shone the solemn Sight.
And thus the Wizard spake with Omens bright;

"Take Office high or low as Days afford,
If One there be that could with thee accord;
Like ancient Kings austere who sought their Mate,
Finding the one who should fulfill their Fate.
Now if thy Heart doth cherish Grace within,
What Need is there to choose a Go-between?
A Convict toiled on Rocks to expiate
His Crime; his Sovereign gave him great Estate.
A Butcher with his Knife made Roundelay;
His King chanced there and happy proved the Day.
A Prince who heard a Cowherd chanting late
Raised him to be a Councillor of State.
Before old Age o'ertake thee on thy Way,

宁戚之讴歌兮,齐桓闻以该辅。

及年岁之末晏兮,时亦犹其未央。

恐鹈鴂之先鸣兮,使夫百草为之不芳。"

何琼佩之偃蹇兮,众薆然而蔽之。

惟此党人之不谅兮,恐嫉妒而折之。

时缤纷其变易兮,又何可以淹留。

兰芷变而不芳兮,荃蕙化而为茅。

何昔日之芳草兮,今直为此萧艾也!

岂其有他故兮,莫好修之害也。

余以兰为可恃兮,羌无实而容长;

委厥美以从俗兮,苟得列乎众芳。

Life still is young; to Profit turn thy Day.
Spring is but brief, when Cuckoos start to sing,
And Flowers will fade that once did spread and
    sping."

On high my Jasper Pendent proudly gleamed,
Hid by the Crowd with Leaves that thickly teemed;
Untiring they relentless Means employed;
I feared it would through Envy be destroyed.
This gaudy Age so fickle proved its Will,
That to what Purpose did I linger still?
E'en Orchids changed, their Fragrance quickly
    lost,
And midst the Weeds Angelicas were tossed.
How could these Herbs, so fair in former Day,
Their Hue have changed, and turned to Mugworts
    grey?
The Reason for their Fall, not far to seek,
Was that to tend their Grace their Will proved
    weak.

I thought upon the Orchids I might lean;
No Flowers appeared, but long bare Leaves were
    seen;
Their Grace abandoned, vulgar Taste to please,
Content with lesser Flowers to dwell at Ease.
To Boasts and Flattery the Pepper turned;
To fill the Pendent Bag the Dogwood yearned;

椒专佞以慢慆兮，樧又欲充夫佩帏。

既干进而务入兮，又何芳之能只？

固时俗之流从兮，又孰能无变化？

览椒兰其若兹兮，又况揭车与江离？

惟兹佩之可贵兮，委厥美而历兹。

芳菲菲而难亏兮，芬至今犹未沫。

和调度以自娱兮，聊浮游而求女。

及余饰之方壮兮，周流观乎上下。

灵氛既告余以吉占兮，历吉日乎吾将行。

折琼枝以为羞兮，精琼蘼以为粻。

为余驾飞龙兮，杂瑶象以为车。

何离心之可同兮，吾将远逝以自疏。

Thus only upon higher Stations bent,
How could they long retain their former Scent?
Since they pursued the Fashion of the Time,
Small Wonder they decayed e'en in their Prime.
Viewing the Orchids' and the Peppers' Plight
Why blame the Rumex and Selinea white?

My Jasper Pendent rare I was beguiled
To leave, and to this Depth then sank defiled.
It blossomed still and never ceased to grow;
Like Water did its lovely Fragrance flow;
Pleasure I took to wear this Bough in Sport,
As roaming wild the Damsel fair I sought.
Thus in my Prime, with Ornaments bedecked,
I roved the Earth and Heaven to inspect.

With Omens bright the Seer revealed the Way,
I then appointed an auspicious Day.
As Victuals rare some Jasper Twigs I bore,
And some prepared, Provision rich to store;
Then winged Horses to my Chariot brought
My Carriage bright with Jade and Ivory wrought.

How might two Hearts at Variance accord?
I roamed till Peace be to my Mind restored.
The Pillar of the Earth I stayed beside;
The Way was long, and winding far and wide.
In Twilight glowed the Clouds with wondrous

邅吾道夫昆仑兮，路修远以周流。

扬云霓之晻蔼兮，鸣玉鸾之啾啾。

朝发轫于天津兮，夕余至乎西极。

凤皇翼其承旂兮，高翱翔之翼翼。

忽吾行此流沙兮，遵赤水而容与。

麾蛟龙使梁津兮，诏西皇使涉予。

路修远以多艰兮，腾众车使径待。

路不周以左转兮，指西海以为期。

屯余车其千乘兮，齐玉轪而并驰。

驾八龙之蜿蜿兮，载云旗之委蛇。

抑志而弭节兮，神高驰之邈邈。

奏九歌而舞韶兮，聊假日以偷乐。

陟升皇之赫戏兮，忽临睨夫旧乡，

Sheen,
And chirping flew the Birds of Jasper green.
I went at Dawn high Heaven's Ford to leave;
To Earth's Extremity I came at Eve.
On phoenix Wings the Dragon Pennons lay;
With Plumage bright they flew to lead the Way.

I crossed the Quicksand with its treach'rous
    Flood,
Beside the burning River, red as Blood;
To bridge the Stream my Dragons huge I bade,
Invoked the Emperor of the West to aid.

The Way was long, precipitous in View;
I bade my Train a different Path pursue.
There where the Heaven fell we turned a Space,
And marked the Western Sea as Meeting-place.
A thousand Chariots gathered in my Train,
With Axles full abreast we drove amain;
Eight Horses drew the Carriages behind;
The Pennons shook like Serpents in the Wind.
I lowered Flags, and from my Whip refrained;
My Train of towering Chariots I restrained.
I sang the Odes. I trod a sacred Dance,
In Revels wild my last Hour to enhance.
Ascending where celestial Heaven blazed,
On native Earth for the last Time we gazed;
My Slaves were sad, my Steeds all neighed in
    Grief,

仆夫悲余马怀兮,蜷局顾而不行。

乱曰:已矣哉!

国无人莫我知兮,又何怀乎故都?

既莫足与为美政兮,吾将从彭咸之所居。

And, gazing back, the Earth they would not
  leave.

Epilogue
Since in that Kingdom all my Virtue spurn,
Why should I for the royal City yearn?
Wide though the World, no Wisdom can be found.
I'll seek the Stream where once the Sage was
  drowned.

东皇太一

吉日兮辰良,穆将愉兮上皇。

抚长剑兮玉珥,璆锵鸣兮琳琅。

瑶席兮玉瑱,盍将把兮琼芳。

蕙肴蒸兮兰藉,奠桂酒兮椒浆。

扬枹兮拊鼓,疏缓节兮安歌,

陈竽瑟兮浩倡。

灵偃蹇兮姣服,芳菲菲兮满堂。

五音纷兮繁会,君欣欣兮乐康。

THE GREAT EMPEROR
OF THE EAST

Lucky the Hour, auspicious is the Day,
When Homage to our Lord on high we pay.
He grasps his long Sword's Hilt in Jasper bound,
The clanging Pendents wrought in Jade resound.
With Jasper Offerings on the Table laid,
We hold the ritual Twigs of precious Jade.
Ochids and Melilotus grace the Rite.
With Cassia Wine and spiced Mead to delight.
We raise the Rod and strike the sounding Urn,
Midst Peace and Mirth both Dance and Song
   return.
Citherns and Flutes the Revelries display,
The Spirit nobly moves in fair Array.
Entrancing Fragrance fills the ritual Hall,
In Symphony the sweet Notes rise and fall,
Our Lord well pleased good Fortune metes to all.

云中君

浴兰汤兮沐芳,华采衣兮若英。

灵连蜷兮既留,烂昭昭兮未央。

謇将憺兮寿宫,与日月兮齐光。

龙驾兮帝服,聊翱游兮周章。

灵皇皇兮既降,焱远举兮云中。

览冀州兮有余,横四海兮焉穷。

思夫君兮太息,极劳心兮忡忡。

THE LADY OF THE CLOUDS

Bathed in sweet Flow'rs and Orchid-scented
　　Dews,
In Robes of Crocus Petals' varied Hues,
The Spirit hov'ring pauses now and stays,
Forever brightly gleams with brilliant Rays,
Within the Deathless Hall she stays alone;
Her glorious Brightness rivals Sun and Moon.
In queenly Robes, Dragons as Steeds to ride,
She soars on Wings to wander far and wide.
Descending now with royal Dignity,
Sudden to pierce the Clouds she mounts on high.
Her Gaze outreaches the wide Continent,
Surpasses the Four Seas and their Extent.
With Longing, thinking of our Queen, we sigh;
with Anguish deep our Hearts yearn grievously.

湘 君

君不行兮夷犹,蹇谁留兮中洲?

美要眇兮宜修,沛吾乘兮桂舟。

令沅湘兮无波,使江水兮安流。

望夫君兮未来,吹参差兮谁思?

驾飞龙兮北征,邅吾道兮洞庭。

薜荔柏兮蕙绸,荪桡兮兰旌。

望涔阳兮极浦,横大江兮扬灵。

扬灵兮未极,女婵媛兮为余太息。

横流涕兮潺湲,隐思君兮陫侧。

桂棹兮兰枻,斲冰兮积雪。

THE GODDESS OF THE XIANG RIVER

Departing not, ling'ring the Maids delay.
What makes you in the River Islet stay?
Graceful and fair, adorned with skilful Craft,
They sail downstream upon the Cassia Raft.
I bid the River's Waves more slowly go,
Command the Water tranquilly to flow;
I wait for her, yet long she doth delay;
Thinking of her my plaintive Flute I play.
Northward in winged Dragon-boat I glide,
And sailing steer my Course the Lake beside.
With Ivy Leaves and Melilotus bound,
Cedar for Oars, Orchids for Flags are found.
I scan the Bay upon the further Shore,
And from the Stream's Expanse the God implore.
The God imploring, ere my Plaint is spent,
The lovely Damsels my Distress lament.
Like ceaseless Stream my Tears continuous flow;
Though longing for my Queen I hide my Woe.
With Cassia Oars, Orchids my Rigging weave,
And yet through Ice and Snow my Craft would

采薜荔兮水中，搴芙蓉兮木末。

心不同兮媒劳，恩不甚兮轻绝。

石濑兮浅浅，飞龙兮翩翩。

交不忠兮怨长，期不信兮告余以不闲！

鼌骋骛兮江皋，夕弭节兮北渚。

鸟次兮屋上，水周兮堂下。

捐余玦兮江中，遗余佩兮醴浦。

采芳州兮杜若，将以遗兮下女。

时不可兮再得，聊逍遥兮容与。

cleave.
My Wish, like plucking Ivy from the Streams,
From Woods desiring Water-lilies seems.

With Hearts at Variance all is Labour lost;
A Love so light lightly away is tossed.
The rocky Stream with shallow Water flows,
The winged Dragon-bark light skimming goes.
Complaining of our Love, his Friendship feigned,
Breaking our Tryst, he pleads himself detained.
At Dawn beside the Stream my Steeds are pressed;
At Eve upon the Northern Shore I rest;
Beneath my Roof the Birds at Night repose,
Before my Hall the winding River flows.
Cast in the Stream my Pendents wrought in Jade,
While on the Shore Jade Offerings are laid.
Bright Crocus Petals from the fragrant Isle
I pluck, and give my Maidens to beguile.
Time passes by, and never comes again;
In carefree Life I shall at Ease remain.

湘夫人

帝子降兮北渚,目眇眇兮愁予。

袅袅兮秋风,洞庭波兮木叶下。

登白薠兮骋望,与佳期兮夕张。

鸟萃兮蘋中,罾何为兮木上?

沅有茝兮醴有兰,思公子兮未敢言。

荒忽兮远望,观流水兮潺湲。

麋何食兮庭中?蛟何为兮水裔?

朝驰余马兮江皋,夕济兮西澨。

闻佳人兮召予,将腾驾兮偕逝。

筑室兮水中,葺之兮荷盖。

THE LADY OF THE
XIANG RIVER

The Queen upon the Northern Shore descends,
And Sorrow to her Eyes more Beauty lends.
The Autumn Breeze sighs as it flutters slow;
The Lake is ruffled, and the Leaves drift low.
I gaze afar amid the Clover white,
At Dusk desiring my Beloved's Sight.
Why are the Birds gathering the Reeds among,
While idly from the Trees the Nets are hung?
Beside the Stream Orchids and Clover grow;
I long for him, but dare not speak my Woe.
Now in the Twilight dim afar I gaze,
And watch the flowing Water's rippling Maze.
Why browses now the Fawn beside our Door?
What brings the River Serpent to the Shore?
At Dawn beside the Stream my Steeds are pressed,
At Eve I ford the River in the West.
My Loved One beckons, bids me not to stay;
I'll urge my Steeds with him to ride away.

A Palace in the River shall be made,

荪壁兮紫坛,播芳椒兮成堂。

桂栋兮兰橑,辛夷楣兮药房。

罔薜荔兮为帷,擗蕙櫋兮既张。

白玉兮为镇,疏石兰兮为芳。

芷葺兮荷屋,缭之兮杜衡。

合百草兮实庭,建芳馨兮庑门。

九嶷缤兮并迎,灵之来兮如云。

捐余袂兮江中,遗余褋兮醴浦。

搴汀洲兮杜若,将以遗兮远者。

时不可兮骤得,聊逍遥兮容与。

Sheltered beneath the Water-lilies Shade;
With Thyme and purple Shells to deck the Wall,
And fragrant Pepper spread within the Hall.
Cassia and Orchid Rafters shall be laid,
With Jasmine Lintels Clover white displayed,
With Ivy Tendrils Curtains we shall spread,
Sheltered by Melilotus overhead.
Our Corner Stone of Jade shall sparkle white,
And Fragrance of Rock-orchids shall delight;
To deck our Lotus Hall shall Vetch be found,
With fresh Azalea Sprigs together bound,
Our Courtyard filled with varied Herbs and fair,
While Flow'rs within our Hall give Fragrance rare.
The Gods will welcome from the Mountain high,
And Angels cloudike will descend the Sky.
Within the Stream I dedicate my Sleeve,
My Garment's Lapel to the River leave.
Plucking the Islet's Crocus Petals gay,
I send them to the Loved One far away.
Time passes by and never comes again;
In carefree Life shall at Ease remain.

大司命

广开兮天门,纷吾乘兮玄云。

令飘风兮先驱,使冻雨兮洒尘。

君回翔兮以下,踰空桑兮从女。

纷总总兮九州,何寿夭兮在予!

高飞兮安翔,乘清气兮御阴阳。

吾与君兮齐速,导帝之兮九坑。

灵衣兮被被,玉佩兮陆离。

一阴兮一阳,众莫知兮余所为。

折疏麻兮瑶华,将以遗兮离居。

老冉冉兮既极,不浸近兮愈疏。

THE GREAT FATE

Behold the Gate of Heaven swings open wide,
While Hosts of Angels down the dark Clouds ride;
The Whirlwinds I command the Course rehearse,
And bid the icy Rain the Dust disperse.
First slowly circling, then descending sheer,
I cross the Sacred Mountains in his Rear.
Myriad the Men within the Cont'nents Nine,
Yet I alone their Span of Life assign.

I soar aloft and circle without Care,
In Light and Darkness through the liquid Air.
With you, oh, Lady of the Clouds, I speed
Through the Nine Continents the Way to lead.
With sacred Garments trailing long displayed,
Of varied Hues my Pendents wrought in Jade.
In Interchange of Darkness and of Light,
My secret Ritual hid from human Sight.
I pluck the giant Flaxes' snowy Head,
An Off'ring to the Lady who has fled.

As old Age nearer draws with ev'ry Day,

乘龙兮辚辚,高驼兮冲天。

结桂枝兮延伫,羌愈思兮愁人。

愁人兮奈何! 愿若今兮无亏。

固人命兮有当,孰离合兮可为?

You should take Pleasure, Lady, while you may.
My Dargon-chariot's rumbling Wheels resound,
As high I drive my Chargers Heaven bound.
My Love awaiting, Cassia Twigs I weave,
With endless Longing mournfully I grieve.
In constant Grieving nought is there to gain;
I vow henceforth from Trespass to refrain.
Man's Destiny is fixed and must prevail.
'Gainst Grief and Parting what can he avail?

少司命

秋兰兮麋芜,罗生兮堂下。

绿叶兮素华,芳菲菲兮袭予。

夫人自有兮美子,荪何以兮愁苦?

秋兰兮青青,绿叶兮紫茎。

满堂兮美人,忽独与余兮目成。

入不言兮出不辞,乘回风兮载云旗。

悲莫悲兮生别离,乐莫乐兮新相知。

荷衣兮蕙带,儵而来兮忽而逝。

夕宿兮帝郊,君谁须兮云之际?

与女游兮九河,冲风至兮水扬波。

THE YOUNG FATE

Mingled with Anise, Autumn Orchids late
In Clusters grow before the Palace Gate;
Green are their Leaves, their tender Sprigs are
   white;
Their Fragrance floods my Senses with Delight.
Each Mortal has a Loved One of his own,
Then why should she, the Goddess, sigh alone?
Fresh spring the Autumn Orchids' tender Shoots;
Green are their Leaves and purple are their Roots.
Young Gallants throng the Palace to Entrance,
But I alone am favoured by her Glance,
Come without Word, she leaves without Farewell,
Her Pennons Clouds, she rides the Whirlwind fell.
For Life to part, no Grief more Pain can move;
No Joy excels the Rapture of first Love.
In Lotus Garb, with Melilotus dight,
Swiftly she comes; as sudden is her Flight.
At Dusk on the Celestial Plain she sleeps,
Among the Clouds her secret Vigil keeps;
Bathed in that Stream from whence the Day

与女沐兮咸池,晞女发兮阳之阿。

望美人兮未来,临风恍兮浩歌。

孔盖兮翠旌,登九天兮抚彗星。

竦长剑兮拥幼艾,荪独宜兮为民正。

begun,
She dries her Hair beneath the rising Sun.
For my Belov'd I wait and long in Vain;
Then sadly to the Breeze I sing this Strain:
"With bright plumed Flags, and Peacock Canopy,
You reach the Comet's Tail, nine Heavens high.
Guarding the Young your Scimitar gleams bright;
You only, Lady, can my Heart delight. "

东　君

暾将出兮东方，照吾槛兮扶桑。

抚余马兮安驱，夜皎皎兮既明。

驾龙辀兮乘雷，载云旗兮委蛇。

长太息兮将上，心低徊兮顾怀。

羌声色兮娱人，观者憺兮忘归。

縆瑟兮交鼓，箫钟兮瑶簴，

鸣篪兮吹竽，思灵保兮贤姱。

翾飞兮翠曾，展诗兮会舞，

应律兮合节，灵之来兮蔽日。

青云衣兮白霓裳，举长矢兮射天狼。

THE GOD OF THE SUN

The bright Sun risen from the Orient
Is on my Wall and Sacred Forest bent.
I curb my Steed and ride at steady Pace,
While Night uncovers and to Day gives Place.
Thunder to Dragon-chariot I bind,
With Clouds as Pennons trailing far behind.
With heavy Sighs I start to climb the Sky,
But still I linger in Uncertainty.
Mortals in Song and Spectacle on Earth,
Their Homes forgetting, revel long in Mirth;
With Flutes and Bells and Clarionets of Jade,
The Urns are sounded and the Pipes are Played.
I see the Wizard, sacred and serene,
Who Circles weaves with magic Plumage green;
They join in Dance, reciting many a Rime,
Accordant with the Rhythm and the Time.
The Sun is shaded by the Angels' Flight.
With dark Cloud-garments and with Rainbows
    bright
To pierce the Dog Star my long Shaft I raise;

操余弧兮反沦降,援北斗兮酌桂浆。

撰余辔兮高驼翔,杳冥冥兮以东行。

56

Then grasp my Bow and home return apace.
From the North Star sweet Cassia Wine I pour;
Under my Reins aloft my Chargers soar;
Eastwards, alone, my Path lies evermore.

河 伯

与女游兮九河,冲风起兮横波。

乘水车兮荷盖,驾两龙兮骖螭。

登昆仑兮四望,心飞扬兮浩荡。

日将暮兮怅忘归,惟极浦兮寤怀。

鱼鳞屋兮龙堂,紫贝阙兮朱宫。

灵何为兮水中? 乘白鼋兮逐文鱼,

与女游兮河之渚,流澌纷兮将来下。

子交手兮东行,送美人兮南浦。

波滔滔兮来迎,鱼邻邻兮媵予。

THE GOD OF THE
YELLOW RIVER

With you I roam within the Waters Nine,
The Winds rise rushing, and the Waves decline;
'Neath foaming Chariot's Lotus Canopy,
On Dragons twain and Serpents we rely.
Climbing the Peak I gaze on ev'ry Side;
My Mind goes out to wander far and wide.
As Ev'ning falls, forgetting to return,
With Longing for the distant Stream I yearn.
Its Dragon Halls with glitt'ring Fish Scales spread,
The purple Palace gleams in pearly Red.
Why lurks the River God beneath the Tides?
Seeking bright Fish, on Tortoise white he rides.
With him between the Islets green I roam,
Where melted Ice comes rushing down with Foam.
Crossing his Hands eastwards departs my Lord;
I leave my Love beside the Southern Ford.
Thus am I borne upon the rippling Tide,
While countless Fishes my Returning guide.

山 鬼

若有人兮山之阿，被薜荔兮带女罗。

既含睇兮又宜笑，子慕予兮善窈窕。

乘赤豹兮从文狸，辛夷车兮结桂旗。

被石兰兮带杜衡，折芳馨兮遗所思。

余处幽篁兮终不见天，路险难兮独后来。

表独立兮山之上，云容容兮而在下。

杳冥冥兮羌昼晦，东风飘兮神灵雨。

留灵修兮憺忘归，岁既晏兮孰华予？

采三秀兮于山间，石磊磊兮葛蔓蔓。

怨公子兮怅忘归，君思我兮不得闲。

THE SPIRIT OF
THE MOUNTAINS

A Presence lingers in the Mountain Glade,
In Ivy and Wistaria Leaves arrayed.
My laughing Lips with gay and sparkling Glance
By sprightly Beauty ev'ry Heart entrance.
With Foxes Train, on tawny Leopards borne,
Jasmine and Cassia Flags my Steeds adorn.
Clad in Rock Orchids, in Azalea decked,
I pluck the fragrant Herbs for my Elect.
Where Reeds gloom darkly and obscure the Day,
Late am I come through steep and weary Way;
I stand alone upon the Mountain's Head,
While multitud'nous Clouds beneath are spread.
The Day is wild, with darkling Gloom increased;
Spirits send Show'rs; Wind blusters from the East.
Delayed by me my Love forgets to leave.
Now the Year wanes, who will my Garlands
   weave?
Within the Mountain magic Herbs I find,
Where clinging Vines the crumbling Boulders bind.
I mourn my Love, forgetting to return.

山中人兮芳杜若，饮石泉兮荫松柏。

君思我兮然疑作。

雷填填兮雨冥冥，猿啾啾兮又夜鸣。

风飒飒兮木萧萧，思公子兮徒离忧。

Kept from his Sight to see him still I yearn.
Midst fragrant Herbs within the Mountain Glade
I drink clear Springs, where Pine and Cedar
   shade.
You think of me, yet still in Doubt remain,
While Thunder rumbles, mixed with Show'rs of
   Rain.
At Night the Monkeys and Hyaenas moan,
By sobbing Winds the rustling Trees are blown,
In vain my absent Lord I mourn alone.

国 殇

操吴戈兮被犀甲,车错毂兮短兵接。

旌蔽日兮敌若云,矢交坠兮士争先。

凌余阵兮躐余行,左骖殪兮右刃伤。

霾两轮兮絷四马,援玉枹兮击鸣鼓。

天时坠兮威灵怒,严杀尽兮弃原野。

出不入兮往不反,平原忽兮路超远。

带长剑兮挟秦弓,首身离兮心不惩。

诚既勇兮又以武,终刚强兮不可凌。

身既死兮神以灵,子魂魄兮为鬼雄!

FOR THOSE FALLEN
FOR THEIR COUNTRY

We grasp huge Shields, clad in Rhinoceros Hide;
The Chariots clash; the Daggers gashing wide;
Flags shade the Sun, like lowering Clouds the
 Foe;
While Arrows fall the Warriors forward go.
They break our Line, our Ranks are overborne;
My left-hand Horse is slain, its Fellow torn;
My Wheels are locked and fast my Steeds become;
I raise Jade Rods and beat the sounding Drum.
The Heav'n grows wrath; the Gods our Fall ordain;
And cruelly we perish on the Plain.
Our Men came forth but never shall return;
Through dreary Plain stretches the Way eterne.
We bear long Swords with curved Bows grimly
 set;
Though cleft the Skull the Heart knows no Regret.
Warlike indeed, so resolute and proud,
Undaunted still and by no Peril cow'd;
Their Spirits deathless, though the Body's slain,
Proudly as Kings among the Ghosts shall reign.

礼 魂

成礼兮会鼓,传芭兮代舞。

姱女倡兮容与。

春兰兮秋鞠,长无绝兮终古。

THE LAST SACRIFICE

The Rites performed the Wizards strike Urn,
Pass round the sacred Herbs and dance in turn.
With Grace the lovely Damsels dance and sing:
"Asters for Autumn, Orchids for the Spring.
Through endless Years this Sacrifice we bring."

惜　诵

惜诵以致愍兮，发愤以抒情。

所非忠而言之兮，指苍天以为正。

令五帝以折中兮，戒六神与向服。

俾山川以备御兮，命咎繇使听直。

竭忠诚而事君兮，反离群而赘肬。

忘儇媚以背众兮，待明君其知之。

言与行其可迹兮，情与貌其不变。

故相臣莫若君兮，所以证之不远。

吾谊先君而后身兮，羌众人之所仇也。

PLAINTIVE LINES

In plaintive Lines to all my Grief
   I give Expression free.
That Everything I say true
   May Heav'n my Witness be!

Five Gods I bid to speak for me,
   Six Deities implore!
Let Hills and Rivers Jury be,
   My Judge the God of Law!

With Loyalty I served my King,
   Till slandered by a Foe.
I would not flatter like the Rest
   As a sage Prince should know.

My Words and Actions stand the Test,
   Nothing has changed in me.
My King may know his Minister,
   The Proof is there to see.

I put my Sovereign's Interest first,
   Hence comes their Enmity!

专惟君而无他兮，又众兆之所仇也。

一心而不豫兮，羌不可保也。

疾亲君而无他兮，有招祸之道也。

思君其莫我忠兮，忽忘身之贱贫。

事君而不贰兮，迷不知宠之门。

忠何辜以遇罚兮？亦非余之所志也。

行不群以巅越兮，又众兆之所咍也。

纷逢尤以离谤兮，謇不可释也。

情沈抑而不达兮，又蔽而莫之白也。

心郁邑余侘傺兮，又莫察余之中情。

固烦言不可结而诒兮，愿陈志而无路。

静默而莫余知兮，进号呼又莫余闻。

申侘傺之烦惑兮，中闷瞀之忳忳。

I serve the Prince with all my Heart,
  So seem their Enemy!

I work unflagging for my Lord,
  But cannot win Success;
My single-hearted Love for him
  Has caused all my Distress.

None serves more loyally than I,
  No Trials can me dismay,
Without a Thought of selfish Gain,
  I scorn the Flatterer's Way.

Though guiltless, I was put to Shame,
  My Counsel overborne.
I never dreamed before that I
  Should be held up to Scorn.

So many Tongues have slandered me,
  To clear myself is hard.
Now crushed, my Voice cannot be heard,
  And from my Prince I'm barred.

My Heart is heavy and cast down,
  None cares for my Distress,
With Griefs too many to recount,
  My Thoughts I can't express.

If I keep silent, no one knows,
  I shout, but none will hear.
In Sorrow and Bewilderment
  My Purpose is not clear.

昔余梦登天兮，魂中道而无杭。

吾使厉神占之兮，曰："有志极而无旁。"

终危独以离异兮，曰君可思而不可恃。

故众口其铄金兮，初若是而逢殆。

惩热羹而吹齑兮，何不变此志也？

欲释阶而登天兮，犹有曩之态也。

众骇遽以离心兮，又何以为此伴也？

同极而异路兮，又何以为此援也？

晋申生之孝子兮，父信谗而不好。

行婞而直不豫兮，鲧功用而不就。

吾闻作忠以造怨兮，忽谓之过言。

九折臂而成医兮，吾至今乃知其信然。

矰弋机而在上兮，罻罗张而在下。

I dreamt that I had scaled the Sky,
　　But halfway up I strayed.
The Demon then foretold my Fate:
　　"You fail for Lack of Aid!"

"And will the Prince forsake me then?"
　　"Do not on him depend.
Much Slander can defile pure Gold,
　　Good Starts may badly end."

When my Attempts proved fruitless all,
　　I should have changed my Way.
Climbing, I kicked the Ladder down,
　　So foolish to this Day.

No Sympathy is shown to me,
　　Yet am I stubborn still.
Even my Friends have left me now,
　　Condemning my Self-will.

There was a filial Prince of Jin
　　Whose Father wronged his Son.
The upright Kun failed in his Task,
　　His Mission was undone.

I heard that Loyalty makes Foes,
　　But thought it could not be;
A Doctor must himself know Pain:
　　So Truth is known to me.

If you soar high, they shoot you down,
　　If low, then Snares are spread;

设张辟以娱君兮,愿侧身而无所。

欲儃佪以干傺兮,恐重患而离尤。

欲高飞而远集兮,君罔谓女何之?

欲横奔而失路兮,盖坚志而不忍。

背应牉以交痛兮,心郁结而纡轸。

捋木兰以矫蕙兮,糳申椒以为粮。

播江离与滋菊兮,愿春日以为糗芳。

恐情质之不信兮,故重著以自明。

矫兹媚以私处兮,愿曾思而远身。

They torture Men to please the Prince—
　　Where can I lay my Head?

To bend my Knee would only bring
　　More Wrath upon my Head.
And if I wander far, my Lord
　　May think that I have fled.

Tempted to give my Passions Rein,
　　My Honour holds me back.
So I am faint and sick at Heart,
　　And all the World looks black.

I gather Melilotus Blooms,
　　And Peppers too I take;
Angelicas and Asters grow,
　　And these my Food will make.

And when I fear my Will is weak,
　　These Verses I repeat,
Rousing myself with fragrant Herbs,
　　I ponder in Retreat.

涉 江

乘鄂渚而反顾兮,欸秋冬之绪风。

步余马兮山皋,邸余车兮方林。

乘舲船余上沅兮,齐吴榜以击汰。

船容与而不进兮,淹回水而凝滞。

朝发枉渚兮,夕宿辰阳。

苟余心其端直兮,虽僻远之何伤!

余幼好此奇服兮,年既老而不衰。

带长铗之陆离兮,冠切云之崔嵬。

被明月兮珮宝璐。

CROSSING THE RIVER

Since I was young I have worn gorgeous Dress,
   And still love Raiment rare,
A long gem-studded Sword hangs at my Side,
   And a tall Hat I wear.
Bedecked with Pearls that glimmer like the Moon,
   With Pendent of fine Jade,
Though there are Fools who cannot understand,
   I ride by undismayed.

Then give me green-horned Serpents for my Steed,
   Or Dragons white to ride,
In Paradise with ancient Kings I'd roam,
   Or the World's Roof bestride.
My Life should thus outlast the Universe,
   With Sun and Moon supreme.
By Southern Savages misunderstood,
   At Dawn I ford the Stream.

I gaze my last upon the River Bank,
   The Autumn Breeze blows chill.

世溷浊而莫余知兮,吾方高驰而不顾。

驾青虬兮骖白螭,吾与重华游兮瑶之圃。

登昆仑兮食玉英,与天地兮同寿,

与日月兮同光。

哀南夷之莫吾知兮,旦余济乎江湘。

入溆浦余儃徊兮,迷不知吾所如。

深林杳以冥冥兮,猿狖之所居。

山峻高以蔽日兮,下幽晦以多雨。

霰雪纷其无垠兮,云霏霏而承宇。

哀吾生之无乐兮,幽独处乎山中。

吾不能变心而从俗兮,固将愁苦而终穷!

I halt my Carriage here within the Wood,
　My Steeds beside the Hill.
In covered Vessel travelling upstream,
　The Men bend to their Oars;
The Boat moves slowly, strong the Current
　sweeps,
　Nearby a Whirlpool roars.

I set out from the Bay at early Dawn,
　And reach the Town at Eve.
Since I am upright, and my Conscience clear,
　Why should I grieve to leave?
I linger by the tributary Stream,
　And know not where to go.
The Forest stretches deep and dark around,
　Where Apes swing to and fro.

The beetling Cliffs loom high to shade the Sun,
　Mist shrouding every Rift,
With Sleet and Rain as far as Eye can see,
　Where low the dense Clouds drift.
Alas! all Joy has vanished from my Life,
　Alone beside the Hill.
Never to follow Fashion will I stoop,
　Then must live lonely still.

接与髡首兮，桑扈臝行。

忠不必用兮，贤不必以。

伍子逢殃兮，比干菹醢。

与前世而皆然兮，吾又何怨乎今之人？

余将董道而不豫兮，固将重昏而终身！

乱曰：鸾鸟凤皇，日以远兮。

燕雀乌鹊，巢堂坛兮。

露申辛夷，死林薄兮。

腥臊并御，芳不得薄兮。

阴阳易位，时不当兮。

怀信侘傺，忽乎吾将行兮。

One Sage of Old had Head shaved like a Slave,
   Good Ministers were killed,
In Nakedness one Saint was forced to roam,
   Another's Blood was spilled.
This has been so from ancient Times till now,
   Then why should I complain?
Unflinchingly still shall follow Truth,
   Nor care if I am slain.

Refrain

    Now, the Phoenix dispossessed,
    In the Shrine Crows make their Nest.
    Withered is the Jasmine rare,
    Fair is Foul, and Foul is Fair,
    Light is Darkness, Darkness Day,
    Sad at Heart I haste away.

哀郢

皇天之不纯命兮,何百姓之震愆。

民离散而相失兮,方仲春而东迁。

去故乡而就远兮,遵江夏以流亡。

出国门而轸怀兮,甲之鼍吾以行。

发郢都而去闾兮,荒忽其焉极。

楫齐扬以容与兮,哀见君而不再得。

望长楸而太息兮,涕淫淫其若霰。

过夏首而西浮兮,顾龙门而不见。

LEAVING THE CAPITAL

High Heav'n proves fickle once again,
And show'rs Calamities like Rain.
Homes are destroyed and loved Ones die,
As East in early Spring we fly.

Now we must wander far and wide,
Eastward, the River as our Guide.
I leave the City sad at Heart,
Forced from my Home today to part.

We leave the Capital behind,
And know not where the Stream may wind.
United Oars the Water cleave;
To see the King no more I grieve.

By Forest Glades I sigh again,
And as I gaze Tears fall like Rain.
East moves the Boat, I dream of West,
Far from the Country I love best.

Now sick at Heart, condemned to yearn,

心婵媛而伤怀兮，眇不知其所蹠。

顺风波以从流兮，焉洋洋而为客。

凌阳侯之氾滥兮，忽翱翔之焉薄。

心絓结而不解兮，思蹇产而不释。

将运舟而下浮兮，上洞庭而下江。

去终古之所居兮，今逍遥而来东。

羌灵魂之欲归兮，何须臾而忘反。

背夏浦而西思兮，哀故都之日远。

登大坟以远望兮，聊以舒吾忧心。

哀州土之平乐兮，悲江介之遗风。

当凌阳之焉至兮，淼南渡之焉如。

曾不知夏之为丘兮，孰两东门之可芜。

I am uncertain where to turn.
By Wind and Current I am borne,
A Stranger drifting all forlorn.

The Stream flows fast, the Boat is sped,
I do not know what lies ahead.
And still my Heart is wracked with Pain,
My Thoughts are like a tangled Skein.

Now downstream all our Vessels row,
Some to the Lake, some East will go.
Leaving our Homes of Yesterday,
To eastern Realms we make our Way.

But still my Soul longs to return,
For that far distant Land I yearn.
My Thoughts still West, still homeward stray.
Grieved that the Distance grows each Day.

To gaze afar, I climb the Hill,
Hoping my aching Heart to still.
The Landscape here is lovely too.
The Valley boasts good Men and true.

The Peasants ask why we have fled,
They have not heard the Tidings dread.
In Ruins lies our royal Town,
The Eastern Gates have toppled down.

心不怡之长久兮，忧与愁其相接。

惟郢路之辽远兮，江与夏之不可涉。

忽若不信兮，至今九年而不复。

惨郁郁而不通兮，蹇侘傺而含慼。

外承欢之汋约兮，谌荏弱而难持。

忠湛湛而愿进兮，妒被离而鄣之。

尧舜之抗行兮，瞭杳杳而薄天。

众谗人之嫉妒兮，被以不慈之伪名。

憎愠恮之修美兮，好夫人之忼慨。

众踥蹀而日进兮，美超远而逾迈。

My Heart is torn and wracked with Pain,
And sad Thoughts follow in their Train,
Far, far removed our City lies,
Hid from our Sight, 'neath distant Skies.

I left the Court when I was spurned,
For nine Years I have not returned.
My Woes too many to express,
Lonely, an Heir to all Distress.

They set themselves to charm the King,
But Favour is a fickle Thing.
Loyal, I would approach the Throne,
But then their envious Arts were shown.

The Virtues of sage Kings gone by
Spread their good Influence to the Sky.
Yet even they were slandered too,
Maligned as impious or untrue.

Goodness and Worth no Praise secure,
But Flatt'rers of Rewards are sure.
While these approach the King each Day,
Good Ministers are turned away.

Refrain
    Exiled, I look back and yearn,

乱曰:曼余目以流观兮,冀一反之何时?

鸟飞反故乡兮,狐死必首丘。

信非吾罪而弃逐兮,何日夜而忘之!

Homeward when shall I return?
To their old Nests Birds will fly,
Foxes face the Hill to die.
Blameless, I was sent away,
Still this rankles, Night and Day.

抽　思

心郁郁之忧思兮，独永叹乎增伤。

思蹇产之不释兮，曼遭夜之方长。

悲秋风之动容兮，何回极之浮浮？

数惟荪之多怒兮，伤余心之忧忧。

愿摇起而横奔兮，览民尤以自镇。

结微情以陈词兮，矫以遗夫美人。

昔君与我诚言兮，曰黄昏以为期。

羌中道而回畔兮，反既有此他志。

憍吾以其美好兮，览余以其修姱。

STRAY THOUGHTS

My Heart with Grief is heavy,
  I sigh with Head down hung.
My Thoughts are like a tangled Skein,
  And yet the Night is young.

In Autumn all Things wither,
  The World is full of Hate,
My Prince is easily enraged,
  And my Affliction great.

The People's Suff'rings move my Heart,
  Our Land I cannot leave.
Here for my Loved One my stray Thoughts
  Into a Song 1 weave.

Oh, once you gave your Promise,
  At Dusk we two should meet;
But then you went back on your Word,
  For such was your Deceit.

You praise another's Beauty,
  Admire another's Grace,

与余言而不信兮,盖为余而造怒?

愿承闲而自察兮,心震悼而不敢。

悲夷犹而冀进兮,心怛伤之憺憺。

兹历情以陈辞兮,荪详聋而不闻。

固切人之不媚兮,众果以我为患。

初吾所陈之耿著兮,岂至今其庸亡?

何独乐斯之謇謇兮? 愿荪美之可光。

望三五以为像兮,指彭咸以为仪。

夫何极而不至兮? 故远闻而难亏。

善不由外来兮,名不可以虚作;

孰无施而有报兮,孰不实而有获?

Forswear your former Pledge to me,
　　And turn an angry Face.

I longed for Reconcilement,
　　But kept by Fear apart,
I dare no more draw near to you,
　　So Grief besets my Heart.

I put my Thought in Verses
　　My Prince disdains to hear,
I know true Worth no Favour wins,
　　And Enemies will sneer.

All that I said was truthful,
　　How could the Prince forget?
By honest Counsel I would make
　　Him more illustrious yet.

I take a Sage as Model,
　　And in his Steps would tread.
I strive for Excellence so that
　　My Prince's Fame may spread.

Virtue is not outside us,
　　Fame springs from noble Deeds,
All Reputations must be won,
　　As Fruit must grow from Seeds.

Interlude

少歌曰:与美人抽思兮,并日夜而无正。

憍吾以其美好兮,敖朕辞而不听。

倡曰:有鸟自南兮,来集汉北。

好姱佳丽兮,牉独处此异域。

既惸独而不群兮,又无良媒在其侧。

道卓远而日忘兮,愿自申而不得。

望北山而流涕兮,临流水而太息。

望孟夏之短夜兮,何晦明之若岁?

惟郢路之辽远兮,魂一夕而九逝。

曾不知路之曲直兮,南指月与列星。

愿径逝而未得兮,魂识路之营营。

何灵魂之信直兮,人之心不与吾心同!

理弱而媒不通兮,尚不知余之从容。

So I plead before my Love,
But his Heart I cannot move.
He approves another's Grace.
In his Heart I have no Place.

Chorus
A Bird flies from the South once more
To the great Stream's northern Shore.
In fair Splendour see him stand,
All alone in a far-off Land;
None to befriend him beneath the Sun,
For Mediators here are none.
Departed long and in Disgrace,
I have no Way to plead my Case.
Beside the Northern Hill I sigh,
My Tears drop where the Stream flows by,
The short Midsummer Nights are here,
Yet each seems long as one whole Year.
The Capital is far away,
But there each Night in Thought I stray
By narrow winding Track or wide,
Southward, with Moon and Stars my Guide,
Forward I press, but all in Vain:
My Soul is weary of such Pain!
Yet still my Nature is too proud
To change or flatter like the Crowd!
For me no one will mediate,
None knows or cares for my sad Fate.

Refrain

乱曰:长濑湍流,沂江潭兮。

狂顾南行,聊以娱心兮。

轸石崴嵬,蹇吾愿兮。

超回志度,行隐进兮。

低佪夷犹,宿北姑兮。

烦冤瞀容,实沛徂兮。

愁叹苦神,灵遥思兮。

路远处幽,又无行媒兮。

道思作颂,聊以自救兮。

忧心不遂,斯言谁告兮!

Long the Bay and strong the Tide,
  As up the Stream I go.
I make my Journey southward still,
  In Hope to ease my Woe.
The Journey here is hard when Cliffs
  Reach steeply to the Sky,
And hard it is to climb or cross
  The Mountain Paths so high.
Brought to a Halt I hesitate,
  And rest here for the Night.
My Mind is clouded, and there seems
  To be no End in Sight.
My Thoughts have travelled far afield,
  In Grief I heave a Sigh,
This Place is strange and desolate,
  No Go-between have I!
My Thoughts in Verses I have set,
  Some Ease of Mind to seek;
But still my Grief is unassuaged,
  For who will hear me speak?

怀　沙

滔滔孟夏兮，草木莽莽。

伤怀永哀兮，汩徂南土。

眴兮杳杳，孔静幽默。

郁结纡轸兮，离愍而长鞠。

抚情效志兮，冤屈而自抑。

刓方以为圆兮，常度未替。

易初本迪兮，君子所鄙。

章画志墨兮，前图未改。

THOUGHTS BEFORE DROWNING

In balmy early Summer Days,
　　When Trees and Grasses teem,
With lonely and dejected Heart
　　I reach the southern Stream.

Now all around appears forlorn,
　　So silent and so still,
While sad and melancholy Thoughts
　　Upon me cast a Chill.

Once more I recollect the Past,
　　And Wrongs of former Days.
Let Others stoop some Gain to win,
　　But I'll not change my Ways.

Such Men as change for selfish Gain
　　I always have despised;
But hold the Principles of Old,
　　The former Rules have prized.

With Sternness and Benevolence
　　An upright Man is filled.

内厚质正兮,大人所盛。

巧倕不斲兮,孰察其揆正。

玄文处幽兮,矇瞍谓之不章。

离娄微睇兮,瞽以为无明。

变白以为黑兮,倒上以为下。

凤皇在笯兮,鸡鹜翔舞。

同糅玉石兮,一概而相量。

夫惟党人之鄙固兮,羌不知余之所臧。

任重载盛兮,陷滞而不济。

怀瑾握瑜兮,穷不知所示。

邑犬群吠兮,吠所怪也。

非俊疑杰兮,固庸态也。

If Craftsmen will not ply the Axe,
　　Men doubt that they are skilled.

You see a Picture in the Night,
　　And black the Colours find.
If skillful Craftsmen squint to see,
　　You need not think them blind.

Now Darkness is construed as Light,
　　And Fair to Foul is turned,
Now Hens and Geese can fly on high,
　　While Phoenixes are spurned.

Now Good and Bad are thought the same,
　　And Jade confused with Stone.
To Men made blind by Prejudice,
　　My Virtues are unknown.

I feel my Task too hard for me;
　　Despairing of Success,
I do not know to whom to show
　　The Jewels I possess.

The country Dogs bark savagely
　　At One they do not know.
And Fools suspect all Men of Worth,
　　And slavish Envy show.

They will not see my Dignity,
　　My Learning or my Grace,

文质疏内兮，众不知余之异采。

材朴委积兮，莫知余之所有。

重仁袭义兮，谨厚以为丰。

重华不可遌兮，孰知余之从容！

古固有不并兮，岂知其何故！

汤、禹久远兮，邈而不可慕。

惩违改忿兮，抑心而自强。

离愍而不迁兮，愿志之有像。

进路北次兮，日昧昧其将暮。

舒忧娱哀兮，限之以大故。

乱曰：浩浩沅、湘，分流汨兮。

修路幽蔽，道远忽兮。

怀质抱情，独无匹兮。

And all my subtle Scholarship
　　Endeavour to abase.

I double my Benevolence,
　　To Honesty I hold;
But who can understand my Worth,
　　Since dead the Sage of Old?

How is it that for such long years
　　The Good remain apart?
The ancient Kings are too long gone
　　To hold them in our Heart.

I curb my Indignation now,
　　My Anger I repress;
I shall not change or hesitate
　　In Danger or Distress.

I journey on and take no Rest
　　Till darkly sinks the Sun.
But now I ease my heavy Heart—
　　My Race will soon be done.

Refrain
　　On and on the Rivers slow
　　Down their several Courses flow.
　　Dark the Way and overgrown,
　　And the Future all unknown.

　　All my Time in Anguish spent,
　　No End set to my Lament
　　By the World misunderstood,

伯乐既没,骥焉程兮。

民生禀命,各有所错兮。

定心广志,余何畏惧兮!

曾伤爰哀,永叹喟兮。

世溷浊莫吾知,人心不可谓兮。

知死不可让,愿勿爱兮。

明告君子,吾将以为类兮。

With no Friend or Kinsman good.

Though my Conscience is quite clear,
I can find no Witness here.
Gone the Charioteer so prized,
The swift Horses are despised.

Sad or happy, each Man's Fate
Overtakes him soon or late.
If I keep a steadfast Heart,
Fear in me can have no Part.

Death, I know, must come to All,
Nor for Mercy would I call.
Saints, I follow in your Wake!
Your Example shall I take!

思美人

思美人兮,擘涕而竚眙。

媒绝路阻兮,言不可结而诒。

蹇蹇之烦冤兮,陷滞而不发。

申旦以舒中情兮,志沈菀而莫达。

愿寄言于浮云兮,遇丰隆而不将。

因归鸟而致辞兮,羌迅高而难当。

高辛之灵晟兮,遭玄鸟而致诒。

欲变节以从俗兮,媿易初而屈志。

独历年而离愍兮,羌冯心犹未化。

LONGING FOR MY LOVE

Lonely, longing for my Love,
I gaze afar in my Distress.
Far from Home and Go-between,
How shall I my Grief express?

My great Loyalty was wronged,
In my Path I hesitate;
Every Day my Case I'd plead,
Every Day lament my Fate.

Clouds I seek as Messengers,
My Petition they deny;
Swallows would swift Envoys make,
Heedless they have flown on High.

One of Old made known his Love
By a Phoenix through the Air.
Should I stoop to change my Way?
Shame compels me to forbear.

I have suffered many a Year,
Wrath consumes me to this Day.

宁隐闵而寿考兮，何变易之可为！

知前辙之不遂兮，未改此度。

车既覆而马颠兮，蹇独怀此异路。

勒骐骥而更驾兮，造父为我操之。

迁逡次而勿驱兮，聊假日以须旹。

指嶓冢之西隈兮，与纁黄以为期。

开春发岁兮，白日出之悠悠。

吾将荡志而愉乐兮，遵江、夏以娱忧。

擥大薄之芳茝兮，搴长洲之宿莽。

惜吾不及古之人兮，吾谁与玩此芳草。

解萹薄与杂菜兮，备以为交佩。

佩缤纷以缭转兮，遂萎绝而离异。

吾且儃佪以娱忧兮，观南人之变态。

Rather though in Anguish die
Than descend to change my Way.

Vanished is the Sage's Way,
Yet still steadfast I remain;
Though the Chariot overturned
Proves my Resolution vain.

Once again I harness Steeds,
Summoning the Charioteer—
Drive on slowly, make no Haste,
Linger a last Moment here—

Pointing at the Western Hill,
Where the River's Source wells clear;
Though we travel on till Night,
Short the Journey will appear.

When the Year is at the Spring,
When the golden Sun shines bright,
I shall wander by the Stream,
Drowning Grief in fresh Delight.

From the Isle pluck Winter-thorn,
Melilotus by the Lake;
Sad that I was born too late,
None my fragrant Herbs will take.

Still I gather fragrant Blooms,
To make up a Pendent gay,
Soon these Flow'rs, now bright and fair,
Withering will fade away.

Longing to forget my Grief,

窃快在其中心兮,扬厥凭而不竢。

芳与泽其杂糅兮,羌芳华自中出。

纷郁郁其远烝兮,满内而外扬。

情与质信可保兮,羌居蔽而闻章。

令薜荔以为理兮,惮举趾而缘木。

因芙蓉以为媒兮,惮褰裳而濡足。

登高吾不说兮,入下吾不能。

固朕形之下不服兮,然容与而狐疑。

广遂前画兮,未改此度也。

命则处幽吾将罢兮,愿及白日之未暮也。

独茕茕而南行兮,思彭咸之故也。

In the strange South I abide,
Here I would abandon Care,
And Resentment set aside.

Fragrance is diffused afar,
From thick Gloom shines Virtue through,
Fame dispels Obscurity,
If your Nature is but true.

I'd beg the Ivy plead my Case,
But I cannot climb the Tree.
Nor will I step into the Lake
To beg the Lilies speak for me.

I do not wish to climb too high.
Nor can I bear to sink too low.
Debasement I cannot endure,
So in Doubt and Grief I go.

Refrain

Longing for an earlier Day,
I shall never change my Way,
Though to Calumny a Prey.
But while still the Sun rides high,
I shall seek a Southern Sky,
Like the Saint of Days gone by.

惜往日

惜往日之曾信兮，受命诏以昭时。

奉先功以照下兮，明法度之嫌疑。

国富强而法立兮，属贞臣而日娭。

秘密事之载心兮，虽过失犹弗治。

心纯庞而不泄兮，遭谗人而嫉之。

君含怒而待臣兮，不清澈其然否。

蔽晦君之聪明兮，虚惑误又以欺。

弗参验以考实兮，远迁臣而弗思。

信谗谀之溷浊兮，盛气志而过之。

RECALLING THE PAST

In Days gone by when, trusted by the King,
The Calendar he bid me to restore,
I taught the People in the ancient Ways,
And codified new Clauses of the Law.

We lived at Peace, our Government was good,
Our Land was wealthy, orderly and strong;
Secrets of State were in my Keeping then,
Nor were small Errors counted a great Wrong.

Then open-handed, circumspect of Speech,
My Fame the Envy of those Flatt'rers drew;
They turned my Prince against me by their Wiles,
And he accepted their Abuse as true.

These Evil-doers wronged our noble King,
Tricked him with Lies to satisfy their Spite.
With no Investigation of the Charge,
How lightly I was banished from his Sight!

My King the evil Slanderers believed,

何贞臣之无罪兮，被离谤而见尤。

惭光景之诚信兮，身幽隐而备之。

临沅湘之玄渊兮，遂自忍而沈流。

卒没身而绝名兮，惜壅君之不昭。

君无度而弗察兮，使芳草为薮幽。

焉舒情而抽信兮？恬死亡而不聊！

独鄣壅而蔽隐兮，使贞臣为无由。

闻百里之为虏兮，伊尹烹于庖厨。

吕望屠于朝歌兮，宁戚歌而饭牛。

不逢汤武与桓缪兮，世孰云而知之？

吴信谗而弗味兮，子胥死而后忧。

And in exceeding Wrath against me turned.
His loyal Subject I shall always be,
Though exiled from his Sight, my Service spurned.

Confronting the dark Waters of the Stream,
I long to drown myself to find Relief,
Destroying at one Stroke both Life and Fame—
My Lord's Deception causes me such Grief.

A loyal Minister and innocent,
They slandered me, hating my virtuous Deeds;
My Prince would not examine into it,
The fragrant Flower hidden by the Weeds.

I long to state my Case before my Lord,
Gladly my Safety to the Winds I'd fling.
But they obstruct a loyal Minister,
Denying me all Access to the King.

A Slave of Old became a Minister,
An honest Kitchen-boy was raised to Fame,
A virtuous Butcher too great Honour won,
A Cowherd's Songs won Office and Acclaim.

Had they not met with Princes good and true,
Who had Discernment worth to recognize,
They would have stayed to all the World
    unknown,
Though talented, who would their Talents prize?

The King of Wu gave Ear to Slanderers,

介子忠而立枯兮，文君寤而追求；

封介山而为之禁兮，报大德之优游；

思久故之亲身兮，因缟素而哭之。

或忠信而死节兮，或訑谩而不疑。

弗省察而按实兮，听谗人之虚辞。

芳与泽其杂糅兮，孰申旦而别之？

何芳草之早殀兮，微霜降而下戒。

谅聪不明而蔽壅兮，使谗谀而日得！

自前世之嫉贤兮，谓蕙若其不可佩。

妒佳冶之芬芳兮，嫫母姣而自好。

虽有西施之美容兮，谗妒入以自代。

愿陈情以白行兮，得罪过之不意。

116

Disaster overtook his Realm apace.
A loyal Subject in the Mountains died,
When the King knew, he swiftly sought the Place.

There on the Mountainside he built a Shrine,
So to repay his Debt of Gratitude,
For he had fed his Sov'reign with his Flesh,
And now he mourned for him whose Death he
   rued.

Some loyal Subjects for their Lord would die,
While wicked Councillors his Favour win.
Our Sovereign will not recognize the Truth,
And fails to see their Falsehood and their Sin.

The Fragrant and the Filthy are confused.
Ah, is there none to differentiate?
And fragrant Herbs have withered quite away,
For they ignored the Frost until too late.

Our King allows himself to be deceived,
So Flatterers and Slanderers abound;
These always have attacked good Ministers,
Eager to throw their Orchids to the Ground.

They envy those who true Distinction show,
And, ugly, still pretend that they are fair.
But all the Artifice of Flatterers
Cannot with honest Loveliness compare.

My Innocence is easy to maintain,

情冤见之日明兮,如列宿之错置。

乘骐骥而驰骋兮,无辔衔而自载;

乘氾泭以下流兮,无舟楫而自备。

背法度而心治兮,辟与此其无异。

宁溘死而流亡兮,恐祸殃之有再。

不毕辞而赴渊兮,惜壅君之不识!

But Sentence fell, and no Appeal had I.
The great Injustice done is clear to All,
Clear as the Stars that twinkle in the Sky.

Like those who rashly throw away their Reins,
And madly on a racing Charger ride,
Or Sailors on a Raft that shoots downstream,
Who have no Oars with which to stem the Tide.

Thus breaking old Traditions at your Whim,
With reckless Rule, Destruction you defy.
Before Disaster overtakes our Realm
I rather choose in Exile here to die.

Refrain

I seek the Stream, and here these Verses leave.
That our King lacks Sagacity I grieve.

橘 颂

后皇嘉树，橘徕服兮。

受命不迁，生南国兮。

深固难徙，更一志兮。

绿叶素荣，纷其可喜兮。

曾枝剡棘，园果抟兮。

青黄杂糅，文章烂兮。

精色内白，类可任兮。

纷缊宜修，姱而不丑兮。

嗟尔幼志，有以异兮。

独立不迁，岂不可喜兮。

ODE TO THE ORANGE

Here the Orange Tree is found,
Shedding Beauty all around.
Living in this Southern Grove
From its Fate it will not move;
For as its Roots lie fast and deep,
So its Purpose it will keep.
With green Leaves and Blossoms white,
It brings Beauty and Delight.
Yet Foliage and sharp Thorns abound
To guard the Fruit so ripe and round.
Golden Clusters, Clusters green
Glimmer with a lovely Sheen,
While all within is pure and clear
Like Heart of a Philosopher.
Grace and Splendour here are one,
Beauty all and Blemish none.

Your youthful and impetuous Heart
Sets you from common Men apart,
And well-contented I to see
Your resolute Integrity.

深固难徙,廓其无求兮。

苏世独立,横而不流兮。

闭心自慎,终不失过兮。

秉德无私,参天地兮。

愿岁并谢,与长友兮。

淑离不淫,梗其有理兮。

年岁虽少,可师长兮。

行比伯夷,置以为像兮。

Deep-rooted thus you stand unshaken,
Impartial, by no Fancies taken.
Steadfast you choose your Course alone,
Following no Fashion but your own.
Over your Heart you hold firm Sway,
Nor suffer it to go astray;
No selfish Wishes stain your Worth,
Standing erect 'twixt Heaven and Earth.
Then let not Age divide us Twain;
Your Friend I ever would remain.
Be noble still without Excess,
And stern, but yet with Gentleness.
Though young in Years and in Complexion,
Yet be my Master in Perfection.
Then Po Yi as your Standard take,
His Virtues as your Model make.

悲回风

悲回风之摇蕙兮,心冤结而内伤。

物有微而陨性兮,声有隐而先倡。

夫何彭咸之造思兮,暨志介而不忘!

万变其情岂可盖兮,孰虚伪之可长!

鸟兽鸣以号群兮,草苴比而不芳。

鱼葺鳞以自别兮,蛟龙隐其文章。

故荼荠不同亩兮,兰茝幽而独芳。

惟佳人之永都兮,更统世以自贶。

眇远志之所及兮,怜浮云之相羊。

THE ILL WIND

An ill Wind tore the Orchid down,
    Resentfully I burn.
A small Thing can such Havoc wreak;
    Whispers to Rumours turn.

I celebrate the ancient Sage,
    Because his Heart was pure.
However many Lies are spread,
    They cannot long endure.

Cattle and Birds seek out their Kind,
    Rank Weeds no Fragrance boast.
While Dragons would their Splendour hide,
    Small Fish will wrangle most.

Secluded, Orchids give their Scent,
    Sweet Plants grow far from Bane.
An honest Mind that's always fair,
    Supreme alway will reign.

My Thoughts have wandered far astray.

介眇志之所惑兮，窃赋诗之所明。

惟佳人之独怀兮，折芳椒以自处。

曾歔欷之嗟嗟兮，独隐伏而思虑。

涕泣交而凄凄兮，思不眠以至曙。

终长夜之曼曼兮，掩此哀而不去。

寤从容以周流兮，聊逍遥以自恃。

伤太息之愍怜兮，气于邑而不可止。

纠思心而以为纕兮，编愁苦以为膺。

折若木以蔽光兮，随飘风之所仍。

存髣髴而不见兮，心踊跃其若汤。

抚珮衽以案志兮，超惘惘而遂行。

岁曶曶其若颓兮，时亦冉冉而将至。

薠蘅槁而节离兮，芳已歇而不比。

Like Clouds that drift along.
My Mind is reeling and bemused,
  But I must make my Song.

With fragrant Herbs I ease my Heart,
  And long for the Elect.
Alone I sigh, and Tears fall down,
  As deeply I reflect.

All Night in Sadness fall my Tears,
  Sleep only comes at Dawn;
Throughout the Watches of the Night,
  So weary and forlorn.

Awake, I wander restless by,
  Prepared to stand the Test;
But I have sighed and mourned too long,
  And now I know no Rest

By Grief and Suffering beset,
  To Misery a Prey,
The Light of Day I would avoid,
  And drift like Smoke away.

What's past can never come again:
  Yet still my Heart is sore,
My Pendents cannot calm my Grief,
  Bemused, I quit this Shore.

But now, with this departing Year,
  My Life will soon be done.

怜思心之不可惩兮,证此言之不可聊。

宁溘死而流亡兮,不忍此心之常愁。

孤子唫而抆泪兮,放子出而不还。

孰能思而不隐兮? 昭彭咸之所闻。

登石峦以远望兮,路眇眇之默默。

入景响之无应兮,闻省想而不可得。

愁郁郁之无快兮,居戚戚而不可解。

心鞿羁而不开兮,气缭转而自缔。

穆眇眇之无垠兮,莽芒芒之无仪。

声有隐而相感兮,物有纯而不可为。

邈漫漫之不可量兮,缥绵绵之不可纡。

愁悄悄之常悲兮,翩冥冥之不可娱。

凌大波而流风兮,托彭咸之所居。

The Clover dies on broken Stem,
  With all its Fragrance gone.

My Heart will not be comforted,
  My Wound cannot be healed.
Rather than still endure such Grief,
  To Death I choose to yield.

Now, like an Exile far from Home
  Or orphan Child, I stray.
Though every Thought brings Suffering,
  I choose the Sage's Way.

I climb the Rocks and gaze afar,
  The Road is lone and long.
No Sight is seen, no Sound is heard,
  Yet gloomy Thoughts still throng.

My Sorrow is too great to end,
  My Grief a tangled Skein,
My Heart is locked, and lost the Key,
  Beset always by Pain.

The Universe is limitless,
  Void Air contains no Form;
Yet Silence now seems palpable,
  Things uncreated swarm.

The Plain extends without an End,
  And boundless is the Air;
As secret Grief gnaws at my Heart,

上高岩之峭岸兮,处雌蜺之标颠。

据青冥而摅虹兮,遂儵忽而扪天。

吸湛露之浮凉兮,漱凝霜之雾雾。

依风穴以自息兮,忽倾寤以婵媛。

冯昆仑以澄雾兮,隐岐山以清江。

惮涌湍之礚礚兮,听波声之汹汹。

纷容容之无经兮,罔芒芒之无纪。

轧洋洋之无从兮,驰委移之焉止。

漂翻翻之上下兮,翼遥遥其左右。

絜滫滫其前后兮,伴张弛之信期。

观炎气之相仍兮,窥烟液之所积。

悲霜雪之俱下兮,听潮水之相击。

My Spirit wanders there.

I climb the rugged Precipice,
    And on the Rainbow ride.
And so, across the azure Sky,
    Right up to Heaven I glide.

I rinse my Mouth with rimy Frost,
    And sip Dew on the Moon.
In Caverns of the Wind I rest,
    But wake to groan too soon.

I lean upon the Western Hill,
    And scan the misty Shore.
I hear the Waves that thunder past,
    I hear the Torrent roar.

From North to South there is no Bound,
    No End from East to West.
Since Lands stretch wide on every Side,
    How know which Way is best?

Uncertain, I toss up and down,
    And fly from Left to Right.
I press ahead, then backward tread,
    Nature directs my Flight.

I sigh before the sultry South,
    And scan the Eastern Haze.
The Western Lake rings in my Ears,
    On snowy North I gaze.

借光景以往来兮，施黄棘之枉策。

求介子之所存兮，见伯夷之放迹。

心调度而弗去兮，刻着志之无适。

曰：吾怨往昔之所冀兮，悼来者之悆悆。

浮江、淮而入海兮，从子胥而自适。

望大河之洲渚兮，悲申徒之抗迹。

骤谏君而不听兮，任重石之何益！

心绲结而不解兮，思蹇产而不释。

I wander in the Sunlight bright,
   And crack my Whip of Gold.
I seek the Hermit's Mountain high,
   Where starved a Saint of Old.

My Resolution is unchanged,
   My Heart no Anguish wrings.
I want to leap into the Waves,
   To join the ancient Kings.

Refrain
   I lament Men's former Greed,
   Selfishness no Good can breed.
   Float I to the Ocean cold,
   Following the Sage of Old.

卜 居

屈原既放，三年不得复见，

竭知尽忠，而蔽鄣于谗。

心烦虑乱，不知所从。

乃往见太卜郑詹尹曰：

"余有所疑，愿因先生决之。"

詹尹乃端策拂龟曰：

"君将何以教之？"

屈原曰："吾宁悃悃款款，朴以忠乎？

将送往劳来，斯无穷乎？

宁诛锄草茅，以力耕乎？

将游大人，以成名乎？

THE SOOTHSAYER

For three long Years endured the Knight's
   Disgrace,
He had no Means to see his Sovereign's Face.
He served his Prince with Skill and Loyalty,
Till Slanderers conspired to bar his Way.
With Thoughts distracted like a tangled Skein,
He knew not where to turn, and Hope seemed
   vain.

To the Diviner then repaired the Knight,
And begged for his Advice in such a Plight.
His Herbs set ready, cleaned his Tortoise Shell,
The wise Man said: "What would you have me
   tell?"

"Shall I work hard and honestly?" he said.
"Or spend my Time in social Calls instsad?
Shall I still drive the Plough and wield the Hoe,

宁正言不讳,以危身乎?

将从俗富贵,以媮生乎?

宁超然高举,以保真乎?

将哫訾栗斯,喔咿儒儿,以事妇人乎?

宁廉洁正直,以自清乎?

将突梯滑稽,如脂如韦,以絜楹乎?

宁昂昂若千里之驹乎?

将泛泛若水中之凫?

与波上下,偷以全吾躯乎?

宁与骐骥亢轭乎?

将随驽马之迹乎?

宁与黄鹄比翼乎?

将与鸡鹜争食乎?

此孰吉孰凶?何去何从?

世溷浊而不清:蝉翼为重,千钧为轻;

黄钟毁弃,瓦釜雷鸣;

谗人高张,贤士无名。

吁嗟默默兮,谁知吾之廉贞?"

詹尹乃释策而谢曰:

"夫尺有所短,寸有所长,

Or to the Great to curry Favour go?
Shall I the Truth, in spite of Danger, speak,
Or cravenly a Life of Pleasure seek?
Remain aloof and prize Integrity,
Or please the Foolish with my Flattery?
Pure and without Reproach shall I remain,
Or mix with those who my Renown may stain?
Hold high my Head like a good racing Steed,
Or chicken-hearted to Temptation cede?
Stay with the Thoroughbreds, though they are
    few,
Or let the common Herd my Will subdue?
Soar with the Skylark to the azure Sky,
Or else with Barnyard Fowls for Insects vie?
Then tell me, Soothsayer, speak now and say:
Which Course is better? Point me out a Way!
In this vile World we live beneath a Blight.
Fluff is thought heavy, metal Weights thought
    light.
Bronze Instruments of Old are cast away,
On earthen Vessels now their Tunes they play.
Now Slanderers are loved, good Men despised,
Alas! By whom is my true Merit prized?"

The Soothsayer then his magic Herbs set down,
And his Request evaded with a Frown.

物有所不足，智有所不明，

数有所不逮，神有所不通，

用君之心，行君之意。

龟策诚不能知事！"

"Some simple Problem the most Skilled defies,
Some Knowledge is kept hidden from the Wise.
To point your Way I cannot undertake,
Nor conjure up the Spirits for your Sake.
Bit you must act according to your Heart.
No Aid can come from my divining Art."

渔 父

屈原既放,游于江潭,

行吟泽畔,颜色樵悴,

形容枯槁。

渔父见而问之曰:

"子非三闾大夫与? 何故至于斯?"

屈原曰:"举世皆浊我独清,

众人皆醉我独醒,是以见放。"

渔父曰:

"圣人不凝滞于物,而能与世推移。

世人皆浊,何不淈其泥而扬其波?

众人皆醉,何不餔其糟而歠其醨?

THE FISHERMAN

*Like "The Soothsayer,""The
Fisherman" could not have been written
by Chu Yuan. Judging by the language it
too was probably written by a native of
Chu not later than the beginning of the
Han dynasty. This poem, again,
provides valuable material for our study
of the poet.*

Chu Yuan, banished, wandered by
the Canglang River. As he walked he
recited poems. Haggard he looked and
thin.

An old fisherman saw him, and
asked: "Are you not the knight Chu
Yuan? What brought you to such a pass?"

"The crowd is dirty," said Chu Yuan,
"I alone am clean. The crowd is drunk, I
alone am sober. So I was banished."

"A wise man shouldn't be too
particular," said the fisherman, "but
should adapt himself to the times. If
people are dirty, why don't you wallow
with them in the mud? If people are
drunk, why don't you drink a lot too?

何故深思高举,自令放为?"

屈原曰:"吾闻之,

新沐者必弹冠,新浴者必振衣,

安能以身之察察,受物之汶汶者乎?

宁赴湘流,葬于江鱼之腹中,

安能以皓皓之白,而蒙世俗之尘埃乎?"

渔父莞尔而笑,鼓枻而去,歌曰:

"沧浪之水清兮,可以濯吾缨;

沧浪之水浊兮,可以濯吾足。"

遂去不复与言。

Why should you think so hard and hold so
aloof that you were banished?"

Chu Yuan said: "They say, after you
wash your hair you should brush your
hat; after a bath you should shake your
dress. How can a man sully his clean
body with the dirt outside? I would rather
jump into the river, and bury myself in
the belly of the fish, than suffer my
cleanliness to be sullied by the filth of the
world!"

The old man smiled and paddled
away, singing:

"When the River Water's clear,
I can wash my Tassels here.
Muddied, for such Use unmeet,
Here I still can wash my Feet."

Then the old man went away, and
spoke no more with him.

招 魂

朕幼清以廉洁兮，身服义而未沫。

主此盛德兮，牵于俗而芜秽。

上无所考此盛德兮，长离殃而愁苦。

帝告巫阳曰："有人在下，我欲辅之。

魂魄离散，汝筮予之。"

巫阳对曰："掌梦。

上帝，其难从。

若必筮予之，恐后之谢，不能复用。" 巫阳

焉乃下招曰："魂兮归来！

去君之恒干，何为四方些？

舍君之乐处，而离彼不祥些。

REQUIEM

By Nature pure, in Innocence intrenched,
I strove for Truth, my Spirit e'er unquenched;
The Prince I served until his virtuous Deeds
Were lost forever 'mid the vulgar Weeds.
Since virtuous Deeds the Gods would not discern,
With bitter Grief his fiery Soul did burn.

Th'ancestral Voice then to the Wizard spake:
"Now guide this Mortal for his Virtue's Sake.
His wandering Soul thou canst divine and guide
Back to his Frame." The Wizard thus replied:
"In Dreams, great Lord, alone lies all my Skill.
Twere hard indeed to execute thy Will.
Though I restore his Soul his Frame may fail,
And all my Pow'r no longer would avail."
Thus he began to call: "O Soul return.
Why roamest thou, thy earthly Frame dost spurn?
Why Joys forsake to meet such Perils fell?

"魂兮归来,东方不可以托些!

长人千仞,惟魂是索些。

十日代出,流金铄石些。

彼皆习之,魂往必释些。

归来兮,不可以托些!

"魂兮归来,南方不可以止些!

雕题黑齿,得人肉以祀,以其骨为醢些。

蝮蛇蓁蓁,封狐千里些。

雄虺九首,往来倏忽,吞人以益其心些。

归来兮,不可以久淫些!

"魂兮归来,西方之害,流沙千里些!

旋入雷渊,靡散而不可止些。

幸而得脱,其外旷宇些。

赤蚁若象,玄蜂若壶些。

146

O Soul return: in East thou canst not dwell.
There Titans live, a thousand Cubits tall,
Who e'er upon the wandering Spirit fall.
There ten successive Suns thou mayst behold,
Their Heat devouring Stone, with Bronze and
  Gold.
The Dwellers there are 'gainst these Forces armed,
But never could thy Soul escape unharmed.
Return, return, Danger attends Delay.

Return, O Soul, in South thou canst not stay.
There live the Blackteeth and the Gaudybrows
Who murder Strangers to fulfil their Vows;
Men's Flesh they sacrifice, their Bones they grind;
There Cobras move like Grass beneath the Wind.
There Foxes huge a thousand Miles hold Sway,
And Serpents with nine Heads that dart and play;
Men they devour to fortify their Pow'r.
Return, return; thou must not stay an Hour.

O Soul return, for perilous the West
Where Quicksands move a thousand Miles sans
  Rest.
If thou within the thundering Pool were tossed,
Thy Soul would scatter, be forever lost.

五谷不生,丛菅是食些。

其土烂人,求水无所得些。

彷徉无所倚,广大无所极些。

归来兮,恐自遗贼些!

"魂兮归来,北方不可以止些!

增冰峨峨,飞雪千里些。

归来兮,不可以久些!

"魂兮归来,君无上天些!

虎豹九关,啄害下人些。

一夫九首,拔木九千些。

豺狼从目,往来侁侁些。

悬人以嬉,投之深渊些。

致命于帝,然后得瞑些。

归来,往恐危身些!

"魂兮归来,君无下此幽都些!

土伯九约,其角觺觺些。

Shouldst thou succeed to fly from such dread
   Ends,
Still stretching far the Wilderness extends;
Red Ants as huge as Elephants are there,
And great black Wasps that might with Gourds
   compare.
There grow no Crops, nor e'en the scantiest
   Weeds,
The People feed on dry and thorny Reeds.
The barren Earth makes all to wilt away,
And Water there is none along that Way;
Return, return, lest thou experience Woe.

"Return, O Soul, to North thou canst not go.
There Icebergs tower as great Mountains high;
A thousand Miles the sharp Snows stinging fly.
So boundless is this vast and wasted Land,
Stretched far and wide, forever without End.
Return, return, nor tarry longer there.

Return, O Soul, nor try the Heavenly Sphere,
Where Tigers guard the Nine Celestial Gates,
To slay each Mortal rash who penetrates.
A Giant with nine Heads inhabits there,
Who with bare Hands nine thousand Woods can
   tear.
There are the Wolves which roam with hostile
   Eyes,
And wandering howl, utt'ring unholy Cries.
As Sport some Mortals hanging high they keep,
Or throw them over Precipices deep.

敦脄血拇,逐人駓駓些。

参目虎首,其身若牛些。

此皆甘人,归来,恐自遗灾些!

"魂兮归来,入修门些。

工祝招君,背行先些。

秦篝齐缕,郑绵络些。

招具该备,永啸呼些。

魂兮归来,反故居些。

"天地四方,多贼奸些。

像设君室,静闲安些。

高堂邃宇,槛层轩些。

层台累榭,临高山些。

网户朱缀,刻方连些。

冬有突厦,夏室寒些。

川谷径复,流潺湲兮。

Until the High King issues his Decree,
The Soul knows nothing of Security.
Return, return, lest Perils overwhelm.

Return, O Soul, nor seek the Nether Realm.
The Keeper of the Hell has nine Tails long,
And on his Head the Horns are sharp and strong,
With Shoulders huge and Hands with Blood
    defiled,
Who would pursue Men like a Charger wild;
Beneath a Tiger's Brow his three Eyes flame,
And mighty as a Bull's his monstrous Frame.
He feeds on human Flesh, and deems it sweet,
Return, return, whence lurking Perils greet.

Return, O Soul, back to thy City Gates;
The Wizard back retreats, and thee awaits.
There are the wicker Basket and the Strings,
And woven Pennon that the Spirit brings;
The magic Instruments stand ready all;
Long wail the Voices, and thy Spirit call.

Return, O Soul, back to thy Land of Birth,
For Death abounds in Heaven and on Earth:
But in thy Chamber where thy Image lies,
All is serene and harbours no Surprise.
There great Halls and their lofty Domes are found,
The rising Porch with Balusters around;

光风转蕙，絜崇兰些。

"经堂入奥，朱尘筵些。

砥室翠翘，挂曲琼些。

翡翠珠被，烂齐光些。

蒻阿拂壁，罗帱张些。

纂组绮缟，结琦璜些。

"室中之观，多珍怪些。

兰膏明烛，华容备些。

二八侍宿，射递代些。

九侯淑女，多迅众些。

盛鬋不同制，实满宫些。

容态好比，顺弥代些。

弱颜固植，謇其有意些。

姱容修态，絙洞房些。

蛾眉曼睩，目腾光些。

With Tow'rs and Terraces beside the Hill,
The Doors with crimson Squares designed with
  Skill;
Thus warm in Winter and in Summer cool,
With many a Streamlet, many a winding Pool;
There Melilotus 'neath the Spring Breeze bright,
And lofty Orchid making Curtseys light.
The Hall we cross to reach the Chamber Door,
Where scarlet gleam the Lintel and the Floor;
The Walls well glazed, adorned with Feathers
  green,
Surround the Couch whereon Jade Clasps are
  seen.
Kingfisher's Plumage woven with Pearls fine
Their Brightness and their varied Hues combine.
And Flag Leaves soft against the Walls are laid,
Silk Canopies spread over them displayed;
There Girdles red, and silken Garments fair,
Adorned with Jasper bright and Jewels rare.

Within that Hall both rich and strange the Sight,
Where Orchids burn upon the Candles bright;
And at thy Pleasure Damsels fair are led,
With girlish Limbs in turn to share thy Bed;
Of noble Birth and peerless Beauty all
With Headdress rich and varied throng thy Hall;
Gentle and fair, and unsurpassed their Charms,
Though frail yet chaste, and pliant in thy Arms.

靡颜腻理，遗视眄些。

离榭修幕，侍君之间些。

"翡帷翠帐，饰高堂些。

红壁沙版，玄玉梁些。

仰观刻桷，画龙蛇些。

坐堂伏槛，临曲池些。

芙蓉始发，杂芰荷些。

紫茎屏风，文缘波些。

文异豹饰，侍陂陁些。

轩辌既低，步骑罗些。

兰薄户树，琼木篱些。

魂兮归来，何远为些！

"室家遂宗，食多方些。

稻粢穱麦，挐黄粱些。

大苦咸酸，辛甘行些。

With Countenance demure and full of Grace,
They throng within to wait for thy Embrace;
Their mothlike Eyebrows and their slender Eyes,
With softest Skin and languorous Looks entice.
E'er in the Terrace or behind the Screen,
Within thy Sight a Damsel fair is seen.

Kingfisher's Plumage green on Canopy
Adorns that lofty Hall with Pillars high;
On scarlet Walls are crimson Panels laid,
The Rafters finely wrought with brilliant Jade;
On high the Ceiling with its well-carved Beams,
Painted with Dragons bright and Serpents, gleams.
Thus, seated in the Hall or Terrace cool,
Thy Vision rests upon the winding Pool,
Where Lotus Flower with Caltrops Blossom
    weaves,
And where Althea waves its purple Leaves.
Warders in Leopard Skin and Garb of State,
Ranged by the Steps their Lord's Approach await;
And when thy Carriage rests upon the Ground,
The Guards on Foot and on their Steeds come
    round.
About the Door tall Orchids make a Bower,
And on the Fence blooms the Hibiscus Flower.

肥牛之腱，臑若芳些。

和酸若苦，陈吴羹些。

胹鳖炮羔，有柘浆些。

鹄酸臇凫，煎鸿鸧些。

露鸡臛蠵，厉而不爽些。

秬粔蜜饵，有餦餭些。

瑶浆蜜勺，实羽觞些。

挫糟冻饮，酎清凉些。

华酌既陈，有琼浆些。

归来反故室，敬而无妨些。

"肴羞未通，女乐罗些。

陈钟按鼓，造新歌些。

涉江采菱，发扬荷些。

美人既醉，朱颜酡些。

嬉光眇视，目曾波些。

被文服纤，丽而不奇些。

Return, O Soul, no more in Exile pine;
Thy dear ones now pay Homage at thy Shrine.
The Feast is laid with Dishes rich and sweet,
Millet and steaming Rice, and early Wheat;
With Salt and Vinegar, and Flavours keen,
Ginger and honeyed Pepper too are seen.
Rich juicy Steaks are to the Banquet brought,
With bitter flavoured Soup together sought;
Then roasted Lamb and Turtle Soup succeed,
And Cane Juice to refresh thee at thy Need;
Swans cooked in Vinegar, wild Ducks a Host,
With succulent black Cranes and wild Geese roast;
With Chickens cooked entire and Tortoise rare,
Delicious to thy Taste, a wonderous Fare.
With Cakes and Honey, sweetened Malt to sup,
And pure Meads mixed within the winged Cup;
The Dregs of Wine well crushed and drunk with
     Icc,
Cool and delicious to a Palate nice.
To Home return, thy Relatives among,
Who do thee Reverence and nurse no Wrong.

Before the Feast is served the Damsels come;
They make new Songs, and play the Urn and
     Drum;
The Lotus and the Caltrops Songs they sing;
O'ercome by Wine they blush and to thee cling.
With shyly amorous Looks and languid wise

长发曼鬋,艳陆离些。

二八齐容,起郑舞些。

衽若交竿,抚案下些。

竽瑟狂会,搷鸣鼓些。

宫庭震惊,发激楚些。

吴歈蔡讴,奏大吕些。

士女杂坐,乱而不分些。

放陈组缨,班其相纷些。

郑卫妖玩,来杂陈些。

激楚之结,独秀先些。

"菎蔽象棋,有六簙些。

分曹并进,遒相迫些。

成枭而牟,呼五白些。

晋制犀比,费白日些。

Their hidden Love now darts forth from their
  Eyes;
In Silk Embroideries a graceful Sight,
Their slender Beauty gives thy Heart Delight;
Well matched their Headdress rich and finely
  made.
With strange Designs and Jewels bright inlaid.
The Damsels young with girlish Limbs then dance
In wanton Measures which their Grace enhance;
They move in Pairs, and each her Skirt lifts high;
So towards the Feasters dance they ever nigh.

The Sound of Flutes and Lyres makes wild Uproar,
The thundering Drums with Echoes urging War;
The Palace trembles, shakes the Dome in Fear,
The Warrior's Hymn doth make a solemn Cheer;
With rustic Songs from Countries by the Sea,
The noble ancient Ode concludes the Glee.
Among the Damsels sit the Guests all down;
Abandons each his Belt and tasseled Crown;
In wanton Wise the Damsels make Display;
The Girl disguised as Warrior wins the Day.
Then Draughts they play, and Chess with Ivory
  wrought,
Divided all in Pairs the Games are fought;
The Die is cast, they call the Gods for Aid;
They revel long until the Day doth fade.

铿钟摇簴，揳梓瑟些。

娱酒不废，沈日夜些。

兰膏明烛，华镫错些。

结撰至思，兰芳假些。

人有所极，同心赋些。

酎饮尽欢，乐先故些。

魂兮归来，反故居些！"

乱曰：献岁发春兮，汨吾南征。

菉蘋齐叶兮，白芷生。

路贯庐江兮，左长薄。

倚沼畦瀛兮，遥望博。

青骊结驷兮，齐千乘。

悬火延起兮，玄颜烝。

步及骤处兮，诱骋先。

抑骛若通兮，引车右还。

与王趋梦兮，课后先。

Some strike the Urn and Knock the Wood Frame
  o'er,
Some play the slanting Lyre and sing once more;
Still Wine they urge, forgetting Night or Day;
Within the bright Lamp burns the Orchid grey.
With Skill and Aptness, as with Fragrance sweet,
They chant the Songs for such Occasion meet;
They drink to crown their Joy and praise the Past.
Return, O Soul, homeward return at last.

Epilogue
And once in early Spring, in Days gone by,
I rode to hunt beneath a Southern Sky.
Angelicas and Dogwoods sprouted green,
My Way stretched far across the Stream was seen.
Then leftward o'er the Lakes and Woods I
  glanced;
Proudly my four black Chargers stamped and
  pranced.
With thousand Chariots thundering around,
They burnt the Woods and passed the Torches
  round;
The Sky grew red, the Slaves pursued my Steed;
So on I rode and let the Slaves succeed.
I curbed my Steed and turned him toward the
  Right
To join the King. My Sov'reign came in Sight.
I urged the Slaves; my Sov'reign drove ahead;

君王亲发兮,惮青兕。

朱明承夜兮,时不可以淹。

皋兰被径兮,斯路渐。

湛湛江水兮,上有枫。

目极千里兮,伤春心。

魂兮归来,哀江南!

The fierce Rhinoc'ros at one Shaft fell dead.

The fiery Orb arose, the Night Star waned,
The Years went past, no Hour could be detained.
Now hidden is the Path where Orchids teem;
Still stands the Maple by the limpid Stream.
A thousand Miles away my Heart doth yearn,
Beyond the Wailing Stream, O Soul return!